THE DAY IS COMING

Life and Work of Charles E. Ruthenberg

TO MARY LEA

Come, join in the only battle wherein no man can fail,
Where whoso fadeth and dieth, yet his deed shall still prevail.
Ah! Come, cast off all fooling, for this, at least, we know!

That the Dawn and the Day is Coming, and forth the Banners go.

—William Morris

THE DAY IS COMING

Life and Work of Charles E. Ruthenberg
1882-1927

by Oakley C. Johnson

NEW YORK
INTERNATIONAL PUBLISHERS

ACKNOWLEDGMENTS

Research for this biography necessitated trips to Cleveland, the city where Ruthenberg was born and grew to maturity; and also to Chicago, Detroit, Philadelphia, Washington, D. C., and other cities; interviews with scores of his surviving relatives, old schoolmates and friends, and close associates in the Socialist and Communist parties.

Numerous people have helped in this work, including those who assisted in research, advised on the first draft of certain chapters, or typed large sections. Thanks are due the relatives and old friends of Ruthenberg, all of whom were cooperative and interested.

Special thanks are due to the Jefferson School of Social Science Library; and the staff of the New York Public Library, who arranged several inter-library loans and made photostats and microfilms of Cleveland labor papers. Assistance was received also from the Cleveland Public Library; the Western Reserve Historical Society, Cleveland; the Ohio State University Library, Columbus; the University of Michigan Library, Labadie Collection, Ann Arbor; the Minnesota Historical Society, St. Paul, Minn.; the Rand School Library, New York; the U. S. Department of Labor Library, Washington, D. C.; and the Library of Congress, General Reference and Bibliography Division, Washington, D. C.

One final note: The publication in 1952 of Wiliam Z. Foster's *History of the Communist Party of the United States* enormously simplified my task in writing the concluding chapters of this book, since it provided a full background for the last eight years of Ruthenberg's life. This enabled me to concentrate, in Chapters 9 and 10, on his personal role in those years.

OAKLEY C. JOHNSON

Summer, 1957
New York

Library of Congress Catalog Card, Number: 57-14538

209

CONTENTS

1

AMERICAN BOY

THE MIDWEST is that part of the United States usually regarded as characteristic of the country as a whole, possessing the manufacturing and business skills of the East and the food-producing powers of the West. The Midwest includes the smokestacks of Chicago, the automobile plants of Detroit, the shipping of the Great Lakes. And the heart of this Mid-America, the geographical center of our industrial empire, is Ohio, the birthplace of Standard Oil and the "Mother of Presidents."

It is of some interest—perhaps only in a sentimental sense—that Cleveland, the chief city of Ohio, was also the birthplace of the man who was to found and, until his death, lead the Communist Party of the United States. He was C. E. Ruthenberg, the son of a dock-worker who lived in the poorer districts of that city.

Charles Emil Ruthenberg was born in Cleveland, Ohio, on July 9, 1882, of German parentage. His father, "Worker August Ruthenberg"—as his name was written on his marriage record—had left Germany earlier that year, February 19, taking with him his wife, Wilhelmina, and eight children. They reached the United States on March 9, and went directly to Cleveland. Charles—the ninth child—arrived four months later.[1]

Ruthenberg was born in a stirring period of American history, at a time of great expansion of capital and great rise in working class organization. In 1882, the year of his birth, the first John D. Rockefeller, a fellow-townsman, organized one of the first big "trusts" of our time, and in that year the second national convention of the Federation of Organized Trades and Labor Unions—which four years later was renamed the American Federation of Labor—met in Cleveland.

In that year, the little-remembered Chester A. Arthur, Republican, was president of the United States. The Republican Party had already forgotten the reason of its own birth and had tossed aside the democratic ideals of Lincoln and the Civil War days: it was already the party of Big Business.

The years immediately before and after 1882, throughout the United States, were years of unprecedented development of organized labor on the one hand and of organized monopoly capital on the other; and there were mighty clashes between them. The Knights of Labor, which was thirteen years old when Ruthenberg was born, waged many industrial battles. The Farmers' Alliance, which was strongly organized in the South and West, supported many of the strikes and boycotts which the Knights of Labor carried on, and started the famous Populist revolt. The Populists and the later People's Party, founded in the late 1880's and the early 1890's, initiated and built up the anti-trust movement which has mainly characterized radical and progressive American politics for generations.

Maturing United States capitalism was driving headlong in the direction of political reaction, headed for what Ruthenberg years later called "industrial despotism." And at the same time labor and progressive forces were fighting for their lives, demanding that the trusts be curbed and democracy expanded. These forces founded May Day in the 1880's, and launched the struggle for the eight-hour working day. The whole significance of Ruthenberg's life was based on his championship of the forces of democracy, and particularly the interests of working people.

In the old country, C. E. Ruthenberg's father, August Wilhelm Ruthenberg, from the Prussian province of Brandenburg, was a cigar-maker by trade and in slack seasons a woodchopper in the forests of Kaiser Wilhelm I. He was thirty-six years old, a widower with five children, when he married Wilhelmina Lau, twenty-eight-year-old servant girl of Berlin, who herself had a little daughter to support.

August was a powerful, impressive man, five feet eleven inches in height, with a black beard and moustache and a calm, self-reliant demeanor. He believed in organized labor, and, in Germany, had voted for the Socialists. Wilhelmina Lau, who became August Ruthenberg's wife on November 26, 1874, was a kind woman, small, blond and blue-eyed. Those who knew her remembered her sweet smile, and her singing round the house as she worked. Unlike her husband, who was not a churchgoer, Wilhelmina was an adherent of the Lutheran Evangelical faith. She bore him two daughters, Louisa and Anna, before the family left Germany.

August Ruthenberg's oldest son, William, had to help support the family while they were still in the old country, in the days of Bismarck, the "Iron Chancellor." It was William who, in the new country, almost half a century later, was to put up his hard-earned money, time and time again, to go bail for his half-brother, Charles, arrested in battles for the working class.

On March 3, 1896—eight years after reaching Cleveland—August Ruthenberg made a Declaration of Intention to become a citizen of the United States. He died before he received his Second Papers. His First Papers were taken out in Cleveland, Cuyahoga County, Ohio. The oldest son, William, took out his citizenship papers independently. When the Ruthenberg family came to Cleveland, they did not find themselves alone. In this expanding trade and industrial center, with a population of 160,146, there were 23,170 German-born or of German descent. Many of them, including some followers of Karl Marx, were political exiles from Prussian tyranny. From 1880 to 1890, mostly due to immigration, the German part of Cleveland's population increased to 39,893. The German socialist, Wilhelm Liebknecht, accompanied by Marx's daughter and son-in-law, Eleanor and Edward Aveling, spoke in Cleveland while on a tour of the United States, in the City Armory, October 31, 1886.

Through central Cleveland winds the deep valley of the Cuyahoga River—"Snake River," in the Indian language. In the flat land west of the Cuyahoga, known in the early days as "Ohio City" and spoken of later as the "West Side," dwelt the factory workers and dock hands. Here the Ruthenberg family found their American home. Some three miles further west was the leisurely twisting Rocky River (now a part of

Cleveland suburbs), on whose broad banks the boy Ruthenberg would soon learn to ramble in spring and summer and soak in the quiet beauty of trees and shadowed water. On the fashionable Heights to the East of the Cuyahoga, and southward, lived the factory owners, the politicians, the rich.

Cleveland's Democratic Traditions

Before the Civil War, Cleveland was outstanding as a center of the fight against slavery. In 1832 the Cleveland Anti-Slavery Society was organized. Because Cleveland was a port on Lake Erie, it "was frequented by runaway slaves on their way to Canada," and became "a principal station of the 'Underground Railway.' "[2] In 1850, at a meeting held in Empire Hall to denounce the Fugitive Slave Law, Clevelanders adopted a resolution not to obey it. And in 1858, Cleveland and other Ohio cities formed a rescuing party of a thousand men who saved the runaway Kentucky slave "John," from the grasp of the Fugitive Law officials, and helped him escape to Canada.

Cleveland was also a center of activity in the struggle for woman's emancipation. Abby Kelley and Lucy Stone, pioneers in the fight for women's rights as well as Abolitionists, addressed large audiences in Cleveland on women's demands for equality. On October 5, 1855, the National Women's Rights Convention was held in Melodeon Hall, to insist on women's right to equal education, the right of married women to own property and be legally protected from wife-beating husbands, the equal right of women to speak from public platforms and to have professional careers and to vote. On November 25-26, 1869, the first National Woman's Suffrage Convention, with delegates from twenty-one states and territories, met in Case Hall, Cleveland, to demand the right of women to vote and to hold office.

The birthplace of Ruthenberg was a little wooden frame house with a picket fence around it, now identified as 2215 West 85th Street, N. W., just off Willard Street. That spring of 1882, when August Ruthenberg and his sons built the house with their own hands, West 85th Street was known as

Florence Street, and the Ruthenberg house was numbered 219. (A dozen years later it became 219 Conover Street; the present number was bestowed in 1905.) The neighborhood at that time was on the edge of town. A mile away was the lake front, with the bathing beaches of Edgewater Park, and, farther east, the docks where August Ruthenberg went to work unloading iron ore.

Every working day, toward nightfall, two-year-old Charles Ruthenberg used to press his sober face against the window pane, watching for his father to come home from work. The little frame house on Florence Street was a working class home, and everybody in it worked as soon as he was able. No sooner had August Ruthenberg and his sons hammered the last nail in the house than the oldest boy, William, who was seventeen, went to work in Gus Shafer's blacksmith shop, and the two biggest girls, nineteen-year-old Emilia and fifteen-year-old Augusta, got jobs as domestic workers. By the time Charles was two, Matilda also had hired out to do housework, leaving only seven-year-old Anna to take care of him. And young Gus, already a dockhand at the age of fourteen, was shoveling the red ore beside his father. August Ruthenberg had to lead young Gus by the hand to keep him from falling asleep when they went to work in the early morning.

At home there was work to do, too, for Mother Wilhelmina and the younger children. The white starched curtains at the windows had to be laundered in water carried from the pump and heated on the cookstove. Sauerkraut, cooked in the kitchen, came from cabbage raised in the backyard garden patch, and salted down in barrels in the back shed. And there was darning and mending, and berry-picking and cutting grapes for the nearby farmers.

On a Saturday night, when little Charles watched out the window, or, holding Anna's hand, went down the dirt walk to meet his bearded father and young Gus, it was no earlier than on any other night. Cleveland longshoremen were at it six days a week, ten hours a day. But Saturday night was the pleasantest time of the week, especially for Charles, because the whole family always came home then to spend Sunday. On

Sunday morning, rain or shine, Ma Ruthenberg would take Louisa and Anna on the long walk to church. In church, as at home, Mrs. Ruthenberg loved to sing. The first music Charles listened to was her hymn singing and that of the Lutheran congregation. Throughout his life, although he himself seldom sang, he was always to be deeply moved by music, especially by group singing. Years later, writing from Sing Sing prison to a friend, he told of his deep delight in choral music, recalling the church singing of his childhood memories.

Pa Ruthenberg never went to church. When urged to go, he used to say, "I know the life of Christ, and I try to follow it, but I don't need to go to church every Sunday to hear it all over again." He preferred to stay home and chat with neighbors or longshoremen friends, or play "Sixty-Six" or pinochle with them and the older boys.

On a September morning in 1888, six-year-old Charles, wearing a white collar and bow tie, sat on the boys' side of the downstairs classroom in the clapboarded Old Lutheran School on Lawn Avenue. His straw-colored hair was parted on the left side above a high forehead and serious blue eyes. C. E. Ruthenberg's education had begun. Charles was pretty well clad, because his mother and his sisters Louisa and Anna took great pains with him. Anna, who was five years older than he and ambitious to become a dressmaker, sewed shirts for him, and kept his stockings darned and his pants mended. Charles, the longshoreman's son, used to play marbles with Eddie Arnold, son of a cabinet maker. Charles was as good at shooting marbles as at his studies, Eddie remembers. "There were four of us boys," Eddie recalls. "One was a carpenter's son, who afterward became a carpenter, and one was a wealthy widow's son, who finally became a farmer, and we all played together. But most of the time, there was just Charles and me." On Saturdays, the boys sometimes played baseball, but more often they went out along the twisting Rocky River to roam through the woods on its flat banks, or go swimming or fishing. On these rambles in the spring they picked blue and yellow violets, yellow adder's tongue, the purplish jack-in-the-pulpit; in the summer, the white water lily and the tiger lily, pink wild roses, and, towards fall, greenish-brown cattails.

Edward Arnold remembers that the Ruthenberg family were "good people and good neighbors." As their school days together drew to a close, the two boys drifted apart. Arnold, who years later became a foreman in an electrical works, never took to politics. "One thing sure, Charles was sincere," he says in tribute to his old school chum. "He didn't go into radicalism out of wanting to be a damn politician." Charles went from childhood games to books. By the time he was twelve he discovered the Cleveland Public Library, and from then on the Library was a part of his life.

Pa Ruthenberg's later years, after he stopped working on the docks, grew into a home life of quiet dignity, especially on Sunday afternoons. The card games still continued, but they were a minor accompaniment to the philosophical discussions August, Sr., carried on with his neighbors. Among the friends always to be found at the Ruthenbergs on Sunday afternoon was the eccentric cobbler, William Bengsch, who made bench-built shoes to order for John D. Rockefeller, Sr. Old Bengsch was well-read in German philosophy; less well-read was August, Sr. Around the big sitting-room table they held symposiums on the ideas of Kant, Fichte, Schopenhauer, Hegel and Schelling, quoted verses from Schiller and Goethe, recalled stories from German folklore. With Bengsch came his wife and his pretty, dark-eyed daughter Margaret, about Charles's age. Mrs. Bengsch chatted with Ma Ruthenberg. Part of the time Charles talked with Margaret; part of the time he listened to his father and Bengsch, or joined diffidently in the conversation.

The Ruthenbergs had an amateur gymnasium in their barn. William and the other half-brothers had put up horizontal bars and acquired a collection of dumbbells, boxing gloves, punching bags and weights while Charles was still a little kid. Now that he was of an age to use them, the older boys had all grown up and were working. Charles would go out to the barn by himself after school and practice daily on the apparatus. This exercise, combined with the long walks he was always taking, developed the powerful physique which was to enable him in later years to work tirelessly in the Socialist and Communist movement and withstand the confinement of jail and prison terms.

Charles Ruthenberg graduated from the Trinity School in June, 1896, just before his fourteenth birthday. What was he going to become? It was a question he thought much about. The minister at Trinity, a Rev. Herman G. Sauer, and his deeply religious mother both wanted him to become a preacher. This appealed to the idealism in the youth. The mother, kindly but insistent, urged him. The Rev. Sauer, who remembers him as "a gentle sort of young man," talked gravely with him. Charles thought that on the other hand he might want to be an engineer. And he had certain doubts about religion. Whatever he was to become, he wanted to go to college, although he had no opportunity even to go to high school. He had been taught that America was the land of opportunity, that he could become anything he wanted. But there was no money for college. Charles got work at low pay in a bookstore in the Old Arcade on Superior Avenue, and here he did a lot of reading.[3] While working at the bookstore, he enrolled in Berkey and Dyke's Business College for a ten month's course in the evening school.[4]

Charles was familiar with his family's old-world tradition, but his whole heart was filled with a love for the traditions of America. The stories of the American Revolution and the Civil War, their meaning in the history of human freedom, fired his imagination. He loved the majestic words, "All men are created equal." Theodore Kretchmar, another schoolmate, remembers, "Charles could name from memory more of the signers of the Declaration of Independence, I think, than anyone living." At the business school, Charles learned bookkeeping, accounting, typing. He worked hard, not only because he liked the work, but because these studies, he felt, were the only door that opportunity had opened for him. He even began to dream of becoming a successful business man. He shared in the illusions of capitalist-minded America at the turn of the century. Just before he was sixteen, Charles tried to get another job. He quit business school and made the wearying round of offices, applying for jobs and being turned down. He was still being educated. He was learning about the door of opportunity.

Meanwhile, August, Sr., became seriously ill of diabetes. Then typhoid set in. He died August 23, six weeks after the boy's sixteenth birthday, and was buried in Cleveland's Monroe Cemetery.

Now Charles had to earn money. He could no longer spend time hunting for an office position. He took what he could get. His brother-in-law, Ernest Brandt, who worked at a carpenter's bench in the factory of the F. E. Zimmerman Picture Molding Company, a subsidiary of the Ohio Picture Molding Company, needed a helper. Charles became a carpenter's helper for ten hours a day at nine dollars a week. For a year and more young Ruthenberg stuck at the carpenter's job in the Zimmerman concern. For a year and more he walked back and forth along the 25-foot bench, trimming and polishing picture molding. The youth managed at last to get the attention of Philip Decumbe, secretary-treasurer of the company. Decumbe transferred him at higher pay to the office, where he remained for another year—till he was past eighteen.

He began to read Elbert Hubbard and other big business ideologists. Hubbard published arty magazines, *The Philistine* and *The Fra,* embellished with biographical essays about artists and writers, and coupled with them his "Little Journeys to the Homes of Great Businessmen," in which he lavished praise on the elder John D. Rockefeller and other tycoons. Charles was influenced for a time by these writings, and shared the prevailing illusions about the "service" that salesmen offer customers and about "carrying messages to Garcia" for the boss.[5] While Ruthenberg had not yet begun to question bourgeois economics, he was already questioning the narrow, outgrown philosophical conceptions that he had inherited from his mother and from his schooling. His weekly trips to the Public Library led him now into non-fiction fields. He was reading Tom Paine, and mulling over in his mind not only what Paine said about fighting for American freedom but also what he said about freeing the human spirit from false teaching. He was reading the sharp, satiric speeches of Robert G. Ingersoll, the essays of Emerson with their insistence on the search for truth, the thought-provoking yarns of Mark Twain. Young Ruthenberg didn't go to church very regularly these days. The trips to the library for more books, and midnight study and Sunday reading, absorbed his spiritual energies.

A Daisy Wedding

In the Ruthenberg home, William the blacksmith was now the man of the house. Bengsch the cobbler still came over of a Sunday, and still talked philosophy—with William and Charles. Margaret Bengsch, grown into a pretty young lady, was a frequent visitor, and quite a friend of Anna. It was Margaret Bengsch who introduced Charles to Rosaline Nickel, his future wife. When Margaret was eighteen, she gave a birthday party at her home, to which she invited her old school chum Rosaline, or Rose, as everyone called her. Rose was the girl young Ruthenberg took home that night. Rose was in many ways a contrast to Margaret. She was smaller, fragile, with a simple and direct gaze in her blue eyes. Young Ruthenberg, who was accumulating the dynamic energy that was to make him a leader of battles, felt that he wanted to take care of her.

Rose, like Charles, was eighteen years old, born June 3, 1882. Like him, she was of German descent and American-born. She had gone through the eighth grade in the public schools. She was the youngest of seven children, and he the youngest of nine. Rose had been brought up in the Reformed —not the Evangelical—Lutheran Church, but she, too, had ceased attending religious services. Charles, with gentle pride, took Rose with him now on his jaunts to Rocky River Valley. They picked delicate blue wild hyacinths and white trilliums, and gorgeous pink moccasin flowers; but much of the time they sat on a grassy bank and read poems from Bryant or Whittier, or stanzas from *The Rubaiyat of Omar Khayyam.*

During his nineteenth year Ruthenberg obtained a better-paying job as bookkeeper and salesman for the Cleveland office of the Selmar Hess Publishing Company. The firm handled such books as *Great Men and Famous Women,* in eight volumes, edited by Charles F. Horne. Ruthenberg soon became delivery and sales manager, with some thirty or forty salesmen working under him through Ohio, Michigan and Indiana. He was to work for the Selmar Hess company approximately eight years —years that would help immeasurably to develop his mind and his administrative abilities. These were the years, too, when he was becoming disillusioned with the world of business, and was learning about socialism.

About the time he got the new job, Ruthenberg and Rose became engaged, although they were not married till four years later. Meanwhile, the youth Ruthenberg had filled out physically into a mature man. He was six feet two inches tall. He took care of his health, drank no liquor, did not smoke, kept up his exercise in the backyard gymnasium. When he was twenty, he could pick up a seventy-pound dumbbell with one hand and hold it above his head at arm's length.

Charles and Rose had a "daisy wedding" at Rose's home, 7913 Ferrell Avenue, on June 29, 1904. The groom himself gathered the daisies in big armloads on his wedding morning in a stroll along Mum Road, near the Rocky River, where he and Rose had walked so often together. To please Rose's family, the wedding was conventional, although both young people had by now broken completely with their church backgrounds. Only their immediate families were present. Charles had a four-day vacation. He and Rose moved at once into a five-room apartment in the Oppman Block, 1113 Detroit Street (Now 7500 Detroit Avenue), near West 75th Street. The young couple who set up housekeeping that summer of 1904 were each twenty-two years old. Every Saturday night, with his pay check, he would bring home a mystery story and a box of chocolates, or a couple of opera or theater tickets. Saturday nights, he and Rose would spend reading and munching candy at home, or listening to music or a play in some downtown auditorium. On Sundays, there were still the rambles along the Rocky River, the reading of poetry under the trees. There was still the gathering of wild flowers, brought home in great bunches. Theodore Kretchmar, his old schoolmate, had also married and with his wife Alice had an apartment in the same building as the Ruthenbergs. On the job at Selmar Hess, Charles found a new friend, MacBain Walker. Kretchmar, Walker, and Ruthenberg were to see much of each other in the next few years.

Daniel, only child of Charles and Rose, was born April 4, 1905. The night Rose went into labor, Charles hurriedly called Alice Kretchmar to stay with her while he went for the doctor. It was a two-mile walk to the doctor's house, with no taxicabs available. By the time he returned with the doctor, the baby was born, bathed and in process of being dressed. Alice, who was herself pregnant at the time, had acted as midwife. Charles Ruthenberg was very proud of his wife Rose and his little son Daniel. He called the baby "Dandy."

One of Daniel Ruthenberg's earliest memories is of the toy streetcar his father made for him. It was a wooden model trolley car, a foot long, complete with little seats, doors and everything. And why a street car? For little Dandy it was a fascinating toy, and he could make believe he was riding in it to work, as his dad rode the real street car. For Charles E. Ruthenberg, it was a symbol of something important going on in the Cleveland of that time. Tom L. Johnson, a Single Taxer, "reform" mayor from 1901 to 1909 and himself a street railway magnate, was during that period waging a battle for municipal ownership of Cleveland's trolley-car system and for a three-cent fare. Ruthenberg, observing the graft and corruption exposed by the mayor's crusading administration, was then an ardent supporter of Tom Johnson.

About the time little Dandy was a year old, the Ruthenbergs moved to another apartment at 8111 Madison Avenue, near West 81st Street, where they were to live for several years. Daniel recalls the books that were in his father's study at this address when he was a youngster—the pictures and mottoes on the walls, the heavy library table his father had made, and the bookstand, also handmade at home, which held the newly bought encyclopedia. "On my father's library wall," says Daniel, "hung his favorite portraits, those of Ralph Waldo Emerson, Henry Wadsworth Longfellow, and Wendell Phillips; on another side were epigrams of Elbert Hubbard; on another, the "creed" of the well-known orator, Robert G. Ingersoll. On his library shelves were the works of the great Americans—Nathaniel Hawthorne, William Cullen Bryant, Edgar Allan Poe, Henry Wadsworth Longfellow, Oliver Wendell Holmes, Henry David Thoreau, Thomas Paine, James Russell Lowell, Washington Irving, Mark Twain and Walt Whitman." Daniel adds: "Instead of merely reading these great Americans, my father believed with them and acted on their principles." Ruthenberg's new friendship with MacBain Walker led his thoughts in new directions. Walker, a salesman under Ruthenberg, was a young man full of challenging ideas. He liked to discuss new theories. The three young couples—the Walkers, the Kretchmars, and the Ruthenbergs—each with a baby growing up, were for two or three years almost inseparable. Nearly every Sunday they got together at one home or another, to talk and argue and read. The young men came to regard themselves as a study club. Charles with his "midwest" sense of humor, dubbed the three "The Huntsmen of Minerva."

Their pursuit of wisdom led them into many bypaths. Ruthenberg, broad-visioned and forthright, had a way of forging ahead straight at a problem till he found the essential truth he was after. Walker, college-trained and facile, peeked and pried into every curious corner of knowledge, and at the same time challenged Ruthenberg with his half-cynical comments on every conventional ideal. Kretchmar—the "phlegmatic Dutchman," as Ruthenberg affectionately called him—trailed along behind the other two, and listened.

For two years they met regularly. They discussed the ideas of Emerson, Thoreau, Walt Whitman. They also discussed religion. MacBain Walker, who had studied for the Methodist ministry, was an atheist and he was not backward in saying so. Sometimes they played cards, and Ruthenberg would join in, although he "always felt he didn't have time," and liked to steer his friends back to the world of ideas. Sometimes they talked shop. Ruthenberg had original opinions about advertising and promotion, and often his ideas were put into practice by his employers.

Politics was in the air in this first decade of the twentieth century, and increasingly as time went on the discussions of the "Huntsmen" turned toward the burning political questions facing the people of Cleveland and of the country as a whole. When the group talked politics, MacBain Walker championed socialism and spoke of Karl Marx, while Ruthenberg, then a Tom Johnson enthusiast and an advocate of reform, argued against socialism and in favor of "individual initiative." Walker was not a member of the Socialist Party, but he had read enough to put up a challenging argument. Ruthenberg, on the other hand, was by this time dead set against the "trusts" and "special privilege," but still clung to the idea of "free enterprise." He argued that if a man works hard he can get ahead. Of course there are millionaires, he said, but a man has a right to what he can get. If people fail, that's their hard luck. He gave as an example of praiseworthy enterprise the founder of the company they worked for, who had started out as a poor immigrant, selling books as they themselves were doing.

In championing socialism, Walker took the "example" that was in everybody's mouth, municipal ownership of the street railways, as advocated by Tom Johnson. Municipal ownership was one of the things Ruthenberg agreed with—at least municipal ownership of street railways. Well, said Walker, advancing the typical though naive argument of many Socialists of the time, wasn't that Socialism? Walker went further. He attacked private ownership of all productive enterprises. He said that the workers in these enterprises were exploited, "robbed," defrauded of the "full product of their toil." Ruthenberg argued vigorously against these new ideas, but even as he argued he was becoming dissatisfied with the blind alley in which each talk ended. There were too many unanswered questions.

The discussions on socialism carried over from home to office. Heated debates took place in the Selmar Hess office, with Walker and Ruthenberg as the principal contestants. The original "Huntsmen" were joined by a half-dozen others. Finally, a more or less formal debate between Walker and Ruthenberg was held right in the Selmar Hess citadel of free enterprise, and by general agreement of the congregated salesmen, Walker, champion of socialism, was awarded the palm. Ruthenberg himself felt that he had been worsted. He went straight to the Cleveland Public Library and got a copy of Karl Marx's *Capital,* Volume One. Years later, when he was on trial for his Communist activities, the prosecutor asked him how it was that he became converted to socialism. "Through the Cleveland Public Library," he answered.

There is a story that the Walker-Ruthenberg debates in the office at last reached the ear of the strait-laced general manager, and cost Ruthenberg his job. At any rate, Ruthenberg left the Selmar Hess Company early in 1908, and went to work in the sales department of the Johns-Manville Roofing Company. When Ruthenberg walked home from the Cleveland Public Library with a volume of Karl Marx under his arm, he had reached the climax of this important transition period in his life. In the middle months of 1908, he began calling himself a socialist, but still argued vehemently in support of Tom Johnson and reform.

2

THEORY INTO ACTION

THE ELECTION YEAR of 1908 was an illuminating experience for 26-year-old Ruthenberg, studying Karl Marx for the first time. The Republican Party put up William Howard Taft of Ohio for President. Theodore Roosevelt, imperialist Republican "trust-buster," had recommended Taft as his successor. Taft in his acceptance speech informed organized labor that injunctions were necessary to keep workers from "injuring" their employers' property. And though the country was only now struggling out of the crisis of 1907, which took place under Republican rule, he warned the people that prosperity would go to the dogs if the Democrats got in. Republican boss Mark Hanna had died in 1905, but his demagogic slogan of the "Full Dinner Pail" was still the propaganda of the Republican machine.

The Democrats for the third time nominated the silver-tongued William Jennings Bryan, who posed as spokesman of the trust-hating Middle West farmers. Bryan's preoccupations were with free trade and the illusion of "free silver," and he ran on a platform that called for a graduated income tax and the direct election of United States Senators, plus a mild reproof to the practice of anti-labor injunctions. His frown at injunctions won for Bryan the backing of Samuel Gompers and the American Federation of Labor. Teddy Roosevelt had stolen Bryan's anti-trust thunder in 1904, but Bryan himself, back in 1896 when he first ran for President, had taken his progressive planks from the Populists. The Populists had polled a million and a half votes in 1892 out of a total popular vote of around twelve million (there was no woman suffrage then), indicating a truly strong political movement. They were a middle-class and agrarian reform party which, in effect, sought to turn history's clock back from monopoly to small-scale capitalism. They feared the rising strength of big business without understanding its nature, and bitterly fought the trusts. They largely represented and helped to keep alive the spirit of democratic rule by the people. In 1896 the bulk of Populist votes swung to Bryan, but by 1908—the last election year that saw a Populist ticket—a great many of the Populists had turned to the Socialist Party.

In the presidential contest of 1904 the Socialist Party—still competing with the older but sectarian Socialist Labor Party—polled nearly half a million votes for Eugene V. Debs. In 1908 the Socialists again had Debs at the head of their ticket and for Vice-President a Cleveland-born union printer named Ben Hanford.[1] Besides being a popular lecturer and writer on socialism, Hanford was creator of the character "Jimmie Higgins" —type of the indefatigable rank and file Socialist. Debs campaigned across the country on the "Red Special,"[2] the expenses of which were paid by collections from town to town, and by workers who rode as "passengers" for a short distance.

Here was a party, Ruthenberg saw at once, that was neither faint-hearted nor petty in its advocacy of reforms and its championship of labor. Its planks included not only the income tax, direct election of senators, the initiative, referendum and recall, independence for the Philippines, condemnation of anti-labor injunctions and of child labor, and advocacy of votes for women, but also the revolutionary demand for socialized ownership of all socially operated industry. When Debs spoke in Cleveland on his national campaign tour, Ruthenberg was greatly stirred. A large crowd had met the "Red Special" at the station and escorted Debs to the Armory. There, eight thousand cheering workers heard him call for a Socialist government.

The year 1908 was the twilight of the fighting career of Single Taxer Tom L. Johnson, street railway magnate and reform mayor of Cleveland from 1901 to 1909. During this time, as reported in Lincoln Steffens' crusading articles, Cleveland got the reputation of being the best-governed city in America. Cleveland's Department of Public Works acquired a municipal electric plant and a munipical garbage disposal plant. The parks were turned into public recreation centers, with children's playgrounds and baseball diamonds. In the spring of 1908 the Tom Johnson "municipal" company bought out Cleveland's street railways. The original owners had promised their men a two-cent-an-hour raise, but Johnson refused to pay it. The men struck. Mayor Johnson appealed for public backing for the good of the city. The Socialist Party of Cleveland, along with trade union leaders, supported the strikers. Ruthenberg supported Johnson.

Ruthenberg thought Tom Johnson was bringing the beginnings of socialism to Cleveland through his municipal ownership scheme. Cleveland workers, it seemed to him, were showing bad judgment, not to say ingratitude, by striking for a few cents a day. In a letter to the Cleveland *Plain Dealer,* May 27, 1908, he set forth this view, and took to task the Socialists, Robert Bandlow and Max Hayes, editors of the Cleveland *Citizen,* a trade union paper. He expressed surprise that an anti-Johnson position could be taken by Socialists. "Mr. Johnson has changed the street railway system in Cleveland," he argued, "from one conducted for the profit of the stockholders only to one conducted in the interests of the whole people." Ruthenberg was not yet really a socialist. He was groping and stumbling. Seeking for clarity through discussion with others, he became a persistent letter-writer to the press. In a reply sent direct to Ruthenberg the very day his letter appeared, Robert Bandlow described Johnson's plan as "municipal *capitalism,*" pointing out that stockholders still got a six percent return on their investment. He chided Ruthenberg for writing on matters he knew "nothing about," and added, "If I were you, I should not attempt to criticize . . . Socialism . . . until I had a fair knowledge of the philosophy." Bandlow concluded his letter with the words, "For the social revolution in our time."

On the following day, as soon as Ruthenberg got Bandlow's letter, he sat down and answered it. He assured Bandlow that he had not intended to criticize *socialism.* In fact, he had been making a study of socialism, he said, and listed "Marx, Schaeffle,

Morris, Bax, etc.," as the authorities he had been reading, along with opponents of socialism "such as Graham and Flint."[3] No, it was not socialism but *local Socialist leaders* he was criticizing, Ruthenberg insisted, for their opposition to what he still looked upon as a socialist beginning. "Tom L. Johnson's 'municipal capitalism' means to me municipal socialism," he wrote, "and it is my hope that municipal socialism may be an entering wedge which will clear the way for that socialism which we both so earnestly desire. . . . Allow me," Ruthenberg went on, "to express my hearty endorsement of the closing paragraph of your letter of yesterday to me, reading, 'For the social revolution in our time.' Had I written this sentence I might have worded it: For the social *evolution,* may it reach socialism in our time; for history, as I read it, allows me no other hope." Ruthenberg was earnest in his search for an understanding of society and a cure for its ills. He was *looking for* socialism, and fumbled around at first. Bandlow replied: "Social evolution is a slow process that may and will be hastened by revolution." His letter gave Ruthenberg just the challenge that he needed. Most important of all, it ended with the words—"you should enroll yourself as a member of the Socialist Party, and with us stand for the social revolution in our time."

Joining the Socialist Party

Early in January, 1909, C. E. Ruthenberg strode to the front of a Socialist meeting in the old hall of the United Trades and Labor Council on Superior Avenue and took the Socialist pledge, as printed on the application card:

"Recognizing the class struggle between the capitalist class and the working class, and the necessity of the working class constituting itself into a political party distinct from and opposed to all parties formed by the capitalist class, I hereby pledge that I have severed my relations with all other parties, and I endorse the platform and constitution of the Socialist Party, including the principle of political action, and hereby apply for admission to said party."

Ruthenberg told a friend, years later, how he came to join

the Socialist Party. He was not actually "recruited" at all: he simply went down to a meeting and asked to be signed up. Announcements of Socialist branch meetings were made in the Cleveland *Citizen,* of which Bandlow was business manager and Max S. Hayes, Socialist National Committee member and leader of the Typogrpahical Union, was editor. Ruthenberg, as it happened, simply picked out the Central Branch meeting from the addresses he found each week in the *Citizen,* and went there. Fifteen other new members joined the Socialist Party in January, 1909, making a total membership in Local Cleveland of 342 for that month. Cleveland was then the second largest local in Ohio, Cincinnati being the largest.

The tumult and the shouting of the presidential elections were over. Taft, big business candidate on the Republican ticket, was the president-elect of the country. And in Cleveland, Tom Johnson, the white-haired boy of the liberals and reformers, had outlived his usefulness and was to go down in defeat before the year's end. Ruthenberg had been learning from these events, and getting ready to take his stand. Now he had taken that stand. He was ready for action.

It is noteworthy that—after the Tom Johnson episode—Ruthenberg, as he moved away from the capitalist ideology he had been taught, never showed the slightest inclination to wander into such by-paths as currency reform or single tax. He was too clear and honest a thinker, and too thorough a student, to let himself fall into intellectual double-talk. Ruthenberg went directly to scientific socialism, rejecting along with the old capitalist ideology all its new disguises. Once Ruthenberg put his hand to this plow, he went straight ahead for the rest of his life. without wavering. He took with him into the Socialist Party his friend, MacBain Walker. His other friend, Theodore Kretchmar, remained behind.

Years later, in a letter to a friend from Sing Sing prison, Ruthenberg was to write: "My greatest impulse always is to transform theory into action." This was Ruthenberg's approach to life. When he pledged himself that January night in 1909 as a member of the working class party, he began to transform socialist theory into action for the people.

At the time Ruthenberg joined the Socialist movement, the Socialist Party was only eight years old. Debs, however, had already been a workers' candidate for president, and was a seasoned leader of workers' struggles. The story of his life, as Alexander Trachtenberg says, is the story of the first real steps in the maturing of the American working class.[4] Debs was born November 5, 1855, in Terre Haute, Indiana, of parents who had been French Alsatian immigrants. At sixteen he was a railway fireman, at twenty a member of the newly organized Brotherhood of Locomotive Firemen, and at twenty-five the Brotherhood's national secretary-treasurer. When he was thirty-eight, he organized the American Railway Union, the first large-scale industrial union in the country. It was his experience as head of this union during the Chicago Pullman strike of 1894, and his reading in and out of jail in the next three years, that made him a Socialist. The strike, as he said, was suppressed by United States court injunctions and United States government troops. Debs helped during the next five years in the aligning of political groupings which in 1901 merged into and became the Socialist Party of America.

In 1908, just before Ruthenberg joined it, the party had 41,751 dues-paying members, 41 per cent of whom were members of trade unions also. In that year, Debs' vote was 424,448, nearly three per cent of the total vote. Debs often spoke in Ohio, and the anti-war speech for which he later went to prison was made there. Ruthenberg, as a Socialist, inherited directly from Debs the fighting traditions and purposes of the American working class movement.

One of the elements of American working class thought which he inherited was its international character. "Patriotism, like brotherhood, must be international and all-embracing to be at all," Debs once said. And his trade union ancestor, William Sylvis, founder of the National Labor Union back in 1866, advocated an international alliance of organized labor.[5] A further element of the Debs legacy was the tradition of fighting for women's rights and against Negro slavery, both tied in with labor's struggle on a broad front. Debs' platform in 1900 had a woman's rights plank; and International Woman's Day—like

May Day—grew out of American labor and Socialist activity (it was established in 1910). Marx declared, "Labor cannot emancipate itself in the white skin where in the black it is branded"; and the American Sylvis warned that if white and black workers did not unite, the "capitalists north and south would foment discord" between them.[6] The "Debs Heritage" contained not only glorious traditions of struggle and achievement, but also elements of weakness in theory and action, and a host of problems to solve. In 1909, however, Ruthenberg was only a beginner in the movement. He had read as much of Marx as was available in English. He had a lot to learn, but he had enthusiasm and energy, and something else—the kind of character that could be steeled in struggle.

On a midsummer evening in 1909, Martha Ruthenberg, wife of Charles' older half-brother August, was strolling down Lorain Avenue, when she noticed a man on a soapbox holding forth at the corner of Clark, with a crowd of people listening. "When I got closer," she told others, "I saw it was Charley, standing there big as life talking to those people." She sent a neighbor girl to tell Ma Ruthenberg. And Ma, unbelieving, came right down to the corner with her little three-cornered handkerchief on her head. Her youngest son was making his first speech, making it in his old home neighborhood, less than a stone's throw from the house in which he had been born. His mother stood there a moment, her hands clasped before her, staring up astonished at her tall and very serious son. "Then," Martha remembers, "she whirled and went straight home!"

Ruthenberg began the most important work of his life among his neighbors, in the place where as a child he had played and gone to school. That summer of 1909 Ruthenberg spoke on street corners quite a few times, and when fall came he began to talk at indoor meetings. One of the old Socialists of that day, August Altenbernd, still treasures a pencilled postcard announcing one of Ruthenberg's first such talks, given September 3, 1909. Addressed to members of the First Ward Branch, the card says: "Comrade C. E. Ruthenberg of Central Branch will address the meeting. Come and bring one or two friends to swell the crowd." In his early speaking for the party, Ruthenberg was far from fluent. He appeared embarrassed and awkward. As a speaker he was decidedly made, not born. But even in his first talks there were qualities that held attention. There was knowledge of what he was talking about, and the earnestness of one who believes in his principles and intends to stand by them. An old Slovak comrade recalls that he met Ruthenberg for the first time in July, 1909, when the latter was first sent as a delegate from his branch to the city's central body. "Ruthenberg was introduced to us as a new comrade as well as a delegate," this Slovak leader remembers. "That same night we elected him recording secretary of the central city body."

Special Problems of Socialism

Early in his Socialist career, Ruthenberg had the *Negro* problem called to his attention. A Negro minister, the Rev. Richard Euell, of Milford, Ohio, wrote to the Ohio *Socialist Bulletin* in February, 1909, suggesting that Negroes could be more rapidly recruited into the party if Socialists would go to them in their churches and point out "the way to freedom and plenty." The Negro, said the Reverend Euell, "belongs to the working class and must be taught class consciousness." While Socialists were in general friendly to Negroes, they had not learned the characteristic of the Negro people as an oppressed minority, nor had the Socialist Party worked out a political approach to the special problems of the Negro people. The Socialist platform of 1908 did not contain a single word referring to Negroes. But in 1908 and 1909, the *International Socialist Review,* published by Charles H. Kerr and Company, Chicago, began to carry articles of varying merit on certain aspects of the Negro question, such as the bestial lynchings and job discrimination. The *Review* printed many articles by writers of Left tendencies.

That first year Ruthenberg was in the Socialist Party there was much discussion on *women*—how to get them to join the party, and whether or not Socialists should fight to get them the vote. The demonstration for suffrage in New York City early in 1908 stimulated the Socialist Convention held that year in Chicago to take action about women's rights. Provision was made for a full-time, paid National Woman's Organizer, and Marguerite Prevey of Akron, Ohio, was given that post. Miss Prevey's duty was to "work for equal, civil and political rights in connection with the Socialist propaganda among women and their organization in the Socialist Party."[7]

This was not the first time that Socialists had supported woman's right to equality. But no organizational steps had been taken before 1908 to carry this message to the women themselves. The 1908 Convention approved a plan of work "to promote the suffrage movement," and recognized that "women's economic and social conditions, and the problems arising therefrom," necessitated special appeals to women.

There were as yet few women members in the party. In an article in the April, 1909, Ohio *Socialist Bulletin,* "The Lone Woman in the Local," Nellie Zeh explained what it was that hindered women from joining a "political party that offered them both political and economic freedom." When a woman joined a branch, Miss Zeh said, she found herself generally alone. "The first thing that greets her is that same capitalist mind of these Socialist men who have invited her to come. . . . Indeed, it is a very embarrassing position for both men and women. They want her there, yet now that she is there, they don't know what to do with her. To make the matter worse, they talk about things of which she has no knowledge, and to smoke or not to smoke is the burden on their minds, while she is wondering whether she had better talk or preserve that lady-like silence so much admired by members of the old parties." The advice this woman gave as to the "best way to meet the lone woman who has the daring" to come to the branch was, "Adopt a simple comradeship-like attitude toward her." She added: "I wonder if you men fully realize what that word 'Comrade' means to us women?"

When Ruthenberg read this appeal by a woman Socialist, he had himself been only four months in the party. He tried to bring his wife Rose into the party with him. But a woman's special problems kept her out at first. She was "wrapped up in little Dandy." She did join, however, in 1912.[8]

There were large national groups in Cleveland, and Ruthenberg always accepted invitations to meet with them. When they held their picnics and national anniversary celebrations, it soon happened that he was regularly the "English speaker" on the program. On June 4, 1910, there were eight English-speaking branches in local Cleveland, and 18 foreign-speaking branches. The latter consisted of three German, four Bohemian and four Polish branches, along with one branch each of Jewish, Finnish, Hungarian, Lettish, Lithuanian, Slovak and Italian comrades. By October 16 there was also a Swedish Socialist Club, which Ruthenberg addressed on that date. An old Hungarian worker on Cleveland's West Side tells how Ruthenberg used to speak at the Hungarian Home, as early as 1910. "He was a leading man among us," this worker recalls proudly, "but when he spoke, he spoke not with authority but like a friend, like one of us. That's what made you feel he was so kind."

When the militant Socialist leader of Germany, Karl Liebknecht, during his tour of the United States, lectured in Cleveland for the German-speaking Socialists, Sunday afternoon, October 30, 1910, it was natural that Ruthenberg should be the announced speaker in English. Karl was the son of Wilhelm Liebknecht, who with August Bebel had founded the German Social Democratic Party a generation before—the same Wilhelm Liebknecht who had toured the United States and addressed a Cleveland audience in 1886 when Ruthenberg was a child of four. It was the younger Liebknecht with whom Ruthenberg now shared the platform. Incidentally, counting members of all national groups, Local Cleveland was said by the *Citizen* of October 22, 1910, to be now the largest Ohio local, with 902 members. This compared with the 342 members the local had had twenty-two months earlier, when Ruthenberg joined.

Despite the fact that the 1908 Socialist Convention under the guidance of Morris Hillquit and Victor Berger had avoided expression of any stand on *trade unions* in the platform, it could not be concealed that Eugene V. Debs, the Socialist Party standard-bearer, was an advocate of industrial unionism. William D. Haywood, leader of the Industrial Workers of the World and member of the Socialist National Executive Committee until 1912, spoke frequently in Cleveland. And the *International So-*

cialist Review kept hammering home the principles of industrial unionism, though with a syndicalist undertone. The craft unions had more numerous spokesmen, nearer home. The Cleveland *Citizen,* Ruthenberg's chief medium of expression in his early party years, was the official organ of the Cleveland Trades and Labor Council, an American Federation of Labor central body. Its editors, Max S. Hayes, Robert Bandlow and David H. Jenkins, the first influential Socialists with whom Ruthenberg became acquainted, were AFL members. Max Hayes was well-known as the leader of the Typographical Union, and on several occasions was put forward nationally by the Socialist trade unionists as their candidate for president of the AFL, in opposition to the perennial candidate, Samuel Gompers. On one occasion (1916), Hayes received as much as one-third of the votes.

While the 1908 platform avoided a stand on the craft versus industrial union debate, it did refer specifically to the attempt of the mine-owners to destroy the militant Western Federation of Miners (now the Mine, Mill and Smelter Workers), declaring that this effort "revealed the existence of a far-reaching and unscrupulous conspiracy by the ruling class against the organizations of labor." In that conspiracy, Haywood and two other union leaders had been kidnapped in Cripple Creek, Colorado, in 1906, taken to Boise, Idaho, and held in prison for a year and a half on a frame-up murder charge.[9] Within the Socialist Party the lines were already being drawn in 1908 and 1909 between the crystallizing Right and Left wings, especially on the question of industrial unionism. The Left favored industrial unionism, the chief example of which at that time was the Industrial Workers of the World. The Right, while professing to be neutral in trade union matters, in practice favored the older, well-established craft unions, most of which were affiliated to the American Federation of Labor.

Fighting for Socialist Principles

Ruthenberg was drawn to socialism at first through his sense of justice and fair dealing, but as he read and observed and played his part in the fight for these aims, he became sharply aware of the underlying struggle in society between rich and poor. He remembered more clearly, now, his father's efforts to feed and clothe his family. When he read Elbert Hubbard's article in the *Fra* praising President Taft for the alleged "smiling prosperity everywhere," he was angry. He sharply listed some "prosperity" items of another kind in a letter to the *Citizen* (March 5, 1910) ironically captioned "Taft Smiles!" "The steel trust pays millions in dividends on watered stock," he wrote, "while its employees live in poverty and squalor, and Taft smiles! Unions fighting to maintain a decent standard of living are fined hundreds of thousands of dollars, and Taft smiles![10] Forty thousand shirtwaist makers strike for better wages, and their pickets are arrested and brutally beaten by the police, and Taft smiles! . . .[11] Men are imprisoned, tortured for demanding the right of free speech at Spokane, and Taft smiles![12] Smile on, Big Bill Taft, smile on; smile on while you may. The workers are not smiling. . . . Now is your time to smile; their time is coming."

In this letter Ruthenberg refers impartially to struggles carried on by both the AFL and the IWW. His primary interest was in labor's *struggles,* whether led by a craft union or an industrial union.

In the middle of 1909, a disagreement arose in the party over a proposal to move the state office from Cleveland, Ohio's largest city, to Columbus, the state capital. Letters in the *Bulletin* warned against "so-called intellectuals" who were trying to "use the Party organization as a means to secure a livelihood." But the membership voted in a referendum to move the state office to Columbus.

Ruthenberg took no direct part in the dispute, though he favored Cleveland as a headquarters. He pondered the rather bitter battle with some surprise, and three months later wrote in the *Citizen*: "The labor movement and the Socialist movement naturally first attract the most aggressive . . . members of the working class, because these are apt to be the first to rebel against unjust conditions. Being made up to a large extent of strong personalities, these organizations will be for a long time the battleground of the individual views of these strong personalities. But those who have the real interest of the working class at heart must learn to sacrifice their own personal views and to accept the will of the majority and work in accordance with that will. They must learn the lesson of solidarity."

Ruthenberg did not yet see clearly that certain hidden anti-working class trends within the Socialist Party made inner-party struggle inevitable. From the very first, however, he took a direction in his thinking and writing which was in line with the developing Left movement. He strove for unity, but always on the basis of a theory which, in his view, aimed straight for socialism.

In taking this Marxist stand, Ruthenberg did not, however, fall into the sectarian fault rather common with Left-wingers of that time of refusing to work for reforms. Neither did he have the equally common sectarian fault of disregarding the progressive traditions of American history.

In a letter to the *Citizen,* June 18, 1910, Ruthenberg urged workingmen to study the Declaration of Independence. Does the present system, he asked, destroy "the right of a majority of the people (the working class) to life, liberty and the pursuit of happiness?" Answering that it does exactly that, he went on: "When the workers as a class realize this . . . a new Declaration of Independence will be written and the right of the people to 'alter or abolish' the present system will be invoked."

A certain Dr. G. C. Ashmun demanded in the Cleveland *Plain Dealer* that a course in ethics be established in the city's public schools in order to "combat the tendency toward anarchy and socialism." Ruthenberg took issue with him.[13] After pointing out the confusion of the terms "anarchy and socialism," he wrote: "The golden rule supposedly expressed the highest code of ethics possible for mankind to attain, and no doubt Dr. Ashmun would agree that no better code of ethics could be taught our school children. It would be interesting to know, in view of this fact, in what way the teaching of the golden rule would combat the tendency toward Socialism." Referring to the *Encyclopedia Britannica's* (9th edition) definition, "The ethics of Socialism are identical with the ethics of Christianity," Ruthenberg went on: "Socialists could ask nothing better than that school children be taught a code of ethics, the application of which would be Socialism."[11]

Occasionally, Ruthenberg relaxed at home with his oldest half-brother, William, over a game of chess, a game they had played together for years. William never avowed himself a Socialist, but he attended lectures and mass meetings, and subscribed to Socialist papers.

Ruthenberg had come to the Socialist Party with a deep love for literature. That his artistic interests went beyond the receptive into the creative is shown by a letter written October 28, 1912, to an Ohio woman Socialist and poet, Ann Minturn, in which he said: "I have written nothing but essays on Socialism since I have been in the Party. Before, I wrote five or six stories, which the publishers regularly returned, and even started a novel, of which three chapters are still extant." When he became a Socialist, Ruthenberg did not bottle up his artistic energies. In the work of the movement he found fulfillment for his creative personality. The American literary heritage he loved became a weapon for him in the long fight for the "cooperative commonwealth" (a term used at that time as a synonym for socialism). Memorable phrases from Lincoln and Paine and Emerson and from the Declaration of Independence, and verses from the British poet, William Morris, appeared naturally in his speeches and writings. He brought artistic vision to the party, but he received as well as gave. The party developed and widened his esthetic understanding. In a thousand directions new doors opened, new horizons blazed. In a letter to the *Citizen* he wrote of the "waste of genius" that takes place under capitalism. The long hours and exhausting labor forced upon working men and women, along with the fear of unemployment and other burdens, "smother any inventive or creative talent" that they may have, he said. Socialism, he declared, is the only way to rescue these great human resources for art and science.[15]

More and more Ruthenberg became a party man. The party more and more absorbed his time and energies. He became identified with the party, and its work became his work. The *Citizen* for July 23, 1910, reports that Ruthenberg was not only recording secretary for the City Central Committee but also press correspondent and member of the auditing committee—all of them volunteer, unpaid jobs—along with being on the official list of "local speakers." He was a delegate to the State Convention which met that year at Columbus, April 30 and May 1. The Convention nominated him as Socialist candidate for state treasurer.

In Cleveland, "C. E.," as he came to be called because of his characteristic signature, "C. E. Ruthenberg," was always present as secretary of the City Central Committee, which met at eight o'clock on the first and third Mondays of each month in Room 2 of the headquarters, 817 Superior Avenue, N. W. There were also the regular meetings of the special committees he served on, and the weekly street corner and Sunday afternoon gatherings he attended and often addressed. Besides these specific tasks there was writing to be done, much of which he took care of at the Socialist headquarters, as well as correspondence, the speakers' class, conferences, plans for picnics, and a hundred other things.

At this time Ruthenberg began more and more at the end of the day to go straight from his job to the Socialist headquarters, and there again plunge into work. Inclination as well as the position of press correspondent made him follow carefully dozens of periodicals, daily, weekly and monthly. The local Ohio Socialist press alone included, besides the *Bulletin* and the *Citizen,* at least eight other papers, among them the Toledo *Arm and Torch,* the Coshocton *Socialist,* the Hamilton *Searchlight,* and the Findlay *Call.* A little later there was also the Warren *Worker.* The New York *Call* was the Socialist Party's outstanding daily newspaper, and a new national paper, the *Coming Nation,* was founded in Washington, D. C., under the editorship of A. M. Simons, former editor of the Chicago *Socialist.* The long-established *Appeal to Reason,* edited by Fred D. Warren, was still popular. In New York one of the earliest working class cultural magazines, *Masses,* began publication in 1911. Ruthenberg read them all.

When the Chicago Socialist Lyceum offered Local Cleveland its choice of six lecture-recitals, the City Central Committee quickly engaged all six, including lectures by N. A. Richardson and George R. Kirkpatrick, nationally-known Socialist speakers, and "An Evening of Music" by the Socialist Quartette Concert

Company. John Spargo, Arthur Morrow Lewis and Lena Morrow Lewis, and many other speakers of the time, both Right and Left wing, found their way in the ensuing months and years to the Socialist forums of Cleveland.

In the 1910 fall elections Ohio led all the states of the Union in the number of Socialist votes cast, with a total of 62,356, as given in the *American Labor Year Book* for 1916 (edited by Alexander Trachtenberg and published by the Rand School of Social Science). Tom Clifford, candidate for governor, received 60,637 votes, and Ruthenberg, candidate for state treasurer, received approximately the same. In his home county of Cuyahoga, Ruthenberg got 5,291 votes. Throughout the country Ohio began to be spoken of as the "Red State." The Ohio Socialist Party had 122 locals and 3,429 dues-paying members.

Interesting to American workers of the present day is Ruthenbereg's championship of unemployment insurance in the Chicago *Daily Socialist,* August 8, 1910:

"The lives of the workers are one constant uncertainty," he wrote. "They know not whether on the morrow an accident may not incapacitate them for further work, or whether illness, often the result of the work they do, may not make it impossible for them to labor, and, if they are lucky enough to escape both these, they have still to fear the loss of their jobs and consequent unemployment. Should they be so fortunate as to have accident, illness and unemployment pass them by, they still have to face the problem of providing for their old age. . . . Of course the capitalist-minded will ask why, in the time of prosperity, the worker does not provide for the time of adversity. Why in the years of health and strength he does not save enough of his earnings to keep him in old age, illness or when accident has laid him low. Yes, why? . . . How can they provide for accidents and illness? *How* can they lay away enough to provide for old age? For them it is a struggle to secure a livelihood *now,* and they can give no thought to the future. And how often are their already low wages cut down by unemployment! They are ready and willing to work in order to secure for themselves food, clothing and shelter, but our crazy industrial system forces them to remain idle."

All this time, in addition to his full political work, Ruthenberg in 1909 and 1910 was earning a living for his family. Since 1908 when he left the Selmar Hess concern, he had been working as a salesman for the Johns-Mansville Roofing Company. In his daily employment he observed the weaknesses of capitalism as a system of economy, and in another *Citizen* letter he described how wasteful was its distributive machinery.

He began by quoting a salesman whom he had overheard (in his own office) complaining to his sales manager: " 'It's getting to be awful,' " the salesman griped. " 'When I was in Illinois a dealer in a small town told me fifteen salesmen had called on him in a single day, and another man told me seven men selling the same line had been in town at the same time.' Think of that!" Ruthenberg commented. "Seven men selling the same kind of goods in one town on the same day! Fifteen salesmen calling on a single dealer in one day! How many thousand more men were there doing the same thing in the thousands of towns and cities in the forty-six states of the Union? [Arizona and New Mexico were not admitted to statehood until 1912.—*OCJ.*] Not only are these men drawn from real production, but their railroad fares and hotel bills must be paid. All this expense is added to the cost of the goods they are selling."

While Ruthenberg was disgusted with mere salesmanship, he was alert to salesmanship methods of reaching the public. An instance is his appeal to Clevelanders who attended Debs' lecture, February 12, 1911, to study socialism. The meeting was announced, to begin with, through triangle-shaped red printed cards hung on doorbells throughout the city. Then when the people arrived at Gray's Armory—in spite of a raging blizzard, according to the Ohio *Socialist Bulletin*—every one of the 1,800 in the audience received "a circular giving a list of the books on Socialism in the Public Library."

3

A SOCIALIST CANDIDATE

THE BIG THING that happened in Cleveland in 1911 was Ruthenberg's campaign against Tom Johnson's man, Newton D. Baker, for mayor. Baker, a Democrat, later to become Woodrow Wilson's Secretary of War, won the election. But Ruthenberg won increased support for the Socialist ticket, getting 8,145 votes, in comparison with 1,266 that had been cast for John G. Willert, Socialist candidate for mayor only two years before.

The Ohio campaign got attention that year from the *International Socialist Review.* The October number devoted an entire page to photographs of "Ohio Socialists in Action," with Ruthenberg prominently featured. An accompanying six-page article said: "Comrade C. E. Ruthenberg . . . knows how to do big things."

Just before the mayoralty campaign, Ruthenberg carried on a fight against the local gas monopoly. In a series of letter-articles in the *Citizen,* beginning October 1, 1910, Ruthenberg gave figures on the increasing cost of gas. Before December came to an end, he called on the City Council to submit the question of a bond issue for a municipal gas plant to a popular referendum. Clevelanders would refuse, he pointed out, to turn over their water department or their public schools to Rockefeller, so why should they let a private concern charge them more for artificial gas than they would pay if they ran their own plant?

In January he warned that Republican Mayor Herman C. Baehr had met with gas company representatives for "ten days of secret negotiations," and made a deal. According to this deal, the company was to get five cents more per thousand cubic feet for artificial gas, with the right to raise the price another nickel in "seven or eight years." It was "time for the people to be on their guard," Ruthenberg wrote in the *Cleveland Citizen.*

By the end of January, the Socialist Party presented a petition with eight thousand signatures asking for a referendum on municipal gas, but the City Council denied it. Soon, however, a referendum was won on another issue, during Ruthenberg's mayoralty campaign. He was nominated to head a full ticket at a city-wide convention held July 2 at Socialist Hall. Two weeks later the *Citizen* carried his really sensational exposé of the street-car company steal, in the usual form of a "Letter to the Editor." Headed "Tayler Grant Amendments," it presented convincing figures showing that the Cleveland City Council had casually signed papers making the street-car owners a gift of more than $12,000,000 of the people's money.

Then the editor of the *Citizen* awoke as a journalist. Ruthenberg's following-up contribution was headlined on page one: "Ruthenberg Explains the $12,000,000 Steal That John Stanley and His Cohorts Want to Slip Over."

The gist of the story was as follows: "Through changing *one word* in the municipal ownership clause of the Tayler Franchise," as Ruthenberg put it, the City Council placed the Cleveland Railway Company in a position to collect $12,000,000 from the people "without giving one cent of value in return." This was done through substituting *capital* for *physical* value in a proposed deal by which the city would buy the street railway system. The Tayler Franchise had been advanced originally to enable the private owners to hang onto the street-car business. It provided, however, that the city might buy the railways at their *physical valuation.* The physical value estimate was based on Tom Johnson's earlier disclosure that a $100 share of street-car stock had only $42 actual value, that is, the capital value was more than double the physical value. But no sooner had the Tayler Franchise been adopted, with this proviso, than the company began angling for amendments, and the City Council yielded: the word *physical* was changed to *capital,* and the company's stockholders stood to get the extra millions. (The Tayler Franchise, as Ruthenberg noted in passing, had allowed a moderate steal to begin with, by letting the company add $3,500,000 as "franchise value" to the actual physical value.) But there was still another fraud in the deal. According to the Franchise, the owners would not be burdened overmuch in making current repairs: they were obligated to keep the property only "in a state of efficiency equal to 70% of the cost of production." In other words at any given time, the street-car system could *actually* be worth only 70% of its original *physical* value.

Ruthenberg's revelation of this piling of fraud on fraud was spread abroad in hundreds of speeches and in tens of thousands of leaflets.[1] A Socialist petition was circulated demanding that the Tayler Franchise amendments be submitted to a vote. Between 12,000 and 13,000 signatures were needed, and, mindful of the fate of the gas-referenedum petition, the Socialists worked harder and got 14,950 qualified signatures, as the *Citizen* reported on August 12. The petition was presented to the City Council, and the Council, willy nilly, had to announce that a referendum would be held. The hard fought referendum lost by a comparatively narrow margin, but the Socialists won great prestige. Never had there been such a stir in a city election since the days of Tom Johnson.

In leading these fights for a city-owned gas plant and street railways, Ruthenberg showed time and again that he was under no illusions either of destroying the trusts or of establishing "socialism" through municipal ownership. In dozens of articles favoring municipal ownership, Ruthenberg—after his interchange with Bandlow two years earlier—never once referred to it as "socialism," or "municipal socialism," although such confusion was common among Socialists of the time. He had grown a lot in those two years, which was only natural, for he regularly discussed with his fellow Socialists the current problems of the Socialist movement, and kept reading away at Marx and Engels. He was emphatic, too, about the impossibility of going back to a pre-monopoly "golden age." What is needed, he kept repeating, is for the trustified industries to be collectively owned and controlled. He endorsed the Socialist slogan of the day: "Let the nation own the trusts." The capitalists were doing the job of consolidating industry; the job of "bringing about collective ownership" would have to be done by the workers.

The Socialists of Cleveland, as of all cities where serious

election work was being done, looked hopefully to the example of Milwaukee, which had elected a Socialist administration in 1910. In fact, they expected too much of Socialist Milwaukee: the Milwaukee administration was functioning, not under socialism, but in a capitalist economy. Furthermore, the Socailist officialdom of Milwaukee, political children of the Right wing leader, Victor Berger, were not the best examples for militant Socialists to follow. It was for all that an important historical fact that the Socialist Party, with the support of the city's trade unions, was able to lead and manage so large a city as Milwaukee, and continue to do so for many years. While reformist in character, the Socialist Milwaukee administration performed many valuable social services and benefited the people. But the Milwaukee Administration received vicious attacks from old-party politicians, and Ruthenberg, who carefully watched the situation, defended it. On February 11, he took the Cleveland *Leader* to task for "maligning Milwaukee's Socialist Government." The paper had assailed the Socialists for supposedly increasing the city's expenses. The *Leader* must have been talking, Ruthenberg suggested, about Cleveland's non-Socialist government, alluding, of course, to the current street-railway grab. When the Cleveland *News* attempted an editorial criticism of Milwaukee's handling of the unemployed, Ruthenberg jibed: "It is really interesting to find a Cleveland newspaper giving editorial attention to the unemployed question." Ruthenberg's understanding of the limitations of a Socialist-controlled municipal government in a capitalist society is shown in his declaration that "until Socialists secure complete political power, they hardly can be held responsible for the weaknesses of the profit system they are trying to abolish." He was steadily developing as a thinking leader: his understanding of Marxism was broadening in the only possible way—through combined study and struggle.

The Election Issues

During the election campaign, Ruthenberg concentrated his fire on his chief opponent, Newton D. Baker, candidate of the

Democratic Party. The reputation of Baker as a liberal reformer was his chief stock-in-trade, and Ruthenberg punctured that reputation by steadily insisting that he live up to it. Baker gave himself out as an advocate of municipal ownership, at least as an "ultimate" proposition. To this, Ruthenberg observed that whenever "there was a prospect of accomplishing something, his [Baker's] advocacy has been in such a still, small voice that no one has heard him. Mr. Baker may 'advocate' municipal ownership," Ruthenberg went on, "but the Party he represents does not." Baker's candidacy, he said, "is a bait to catch the unwary radical voter."

In the course of the campaign Newton Baker himself was asked to sign the Socialist petition calling for a referendum on the street-car franchise amendments. Baker got out of it by saying, "I'm for any kind of referendum and I'd like to sign this one, but some folks might say that the Democratic organization is helping fight for a referendum." Ruthenberg wouldn't let him off with this excuse. He asked again, on August 4, why Baker, "a professed advocate of municipal ownership," had not, up to that date, "uttered a single word against the Tayler Grant amendments." Ruthenberg's own answer was that "The stock of the Forest City Railway Company [included in that of the Cleveland Railway Company.—O. C. J.] was owned largely by Democratic politicians and capitalists close to the Democratic organization." Baker's evasion, Ruthenberg indicated, put him "in that class of office-seekers who are willing to sacrifice any material interest of the community" to get into office.

In an open letter to Baker (*Citizen,* September 16), Ruthenberg challenged him to debate the election issue, saying he had "no doubt" that Baker desired "to give the voters of the city the fullest information" as to his stand on matters of vital importance to them. But the elusive Baker declined on the ground that such a debate would "obscure" the issues. Writing on "Make-Believe Radicalism," later that month, Ruthenberg warned against the demagogic users of radical phrases. "Newton D. Baker endeavors to give the impression," Ruthenberg wrote, "that the only differences between him and the Socialists are 'differences of opinion upon questions of method rather than questions of principle.' He seeks to make the working class of Cleveland believe that by electing a candidate of the Democratic Party who uses the phrase, 'that the workers should receive all they produce,' they will move toward the abolition of exploitation."

Later events proved Ruthenberg was right. On October 14, with election day around the corner, the *Citizen* disclosed in an editorial that Newton Baker, "after a long and painful silence," had taken a stand on the Tayler Franchise amendments—by endorsing them. Two days after he did so, the editorial said, the Cleveland Chamber of Commerce endorsed Baker; and Baker himself, at a dinner of bigwigs, warned against the danger of socialism.

Ruthenberg summed up the election issues as follows:[2] "There are two concrete issues before the people of this city today which overshadow everything else in . . . municipal affairs.

"The first is the open and brutal use of the Police Department to intimidate and beat into submission the 6,000 garment workers who are fighting for a greater share of the product of their labor. . . . The second is the $12,000,000 street railway franchise steal put through by the Republican administration, on which the Socialist Party has forced a referendum, and in regard to which there has been a conspiracy of silence on the part of the newspapers of this city."

The five-months strike of Cleveland garment workers in the summer of 1911 was a landmark in American working class history. The leaders of the International Ladies' Garment Workers decided, after a survey of conditions in various cities, to make Cleveland the scene of a strike of workers in the clothing trades. "Cleveland was chosen as the battleground for the beginning of the campaign for two reasons," states *The Women's Garment Workers,* a history of the International Ladies' Garment Workers by Dr. Louis Levine. "One was economic. Though Cleveland at that time ranked fourth in the manufacture of women's clothing in the country . . . it was second only to New York as a cloak and suit market. and had more competitive importance for New York than other cities. . . . At the time the strike was called, there were in Cleveland thirty-three firms which employed 5,000 workers." The history goes on to say that "The other reason for choosing Cleveland was psychologic." Cleveland workers were becoming more and more insistent in their demand for a strike. Tailors averaged from $8 to $15 in weekly earnings; cutters and pressers from $10 to $18 a week, and "The women in the trade, who formed about one-third of the total number of employees, earned from $3 to $12 a week."

The strike started June 6, and continued almost until election day. The strikers' modest demands included a maximum fifty-hour week, with no more than two hours overtime a day for no more than five days a week. They also asked for a Saturday half-holiday and the observance of legal holidays, for joint price committees with employee representation, and for the abolition of inside subcontracting (sweat shop system), as well as a raise in pay. The Socialist Party of Cleveland energetically supported the garment workers. Its City Central Committee adopted an angry resolution of protest against the hiring of armed guards to terrorize the strikers, and called on the city's public officials to disarm all company thugs. By July 15, the *Citizen* reported, Ruthenberg and other speakers were holding street meetings twice weekly in the strike district in the Fifteenth Ward.

On Sunday, September 3, at a huge Labor Day rally in Luna Park sponsored by the trade unions, all mayoralty candidates were invited by the strikers to answer the question, "What would you do, if elected Mayor, to settle the garment workers' strike?" The vote of five thousand garment strikers and of other thousands of sympathizing trade unionists was not to be laughed at, and all the candidates were there.

As reported in the *Citizen* of September 9, Ruthenberg answered the question this way: "The Socialist Party . . . would use the political power it held to help the workers win this strike." He went on to say that the Socialists would "pick out a hundred of the coolest heads among the strikers," and "swear them in as special police" to protect the workers on strike, keep the scabs out, and maintain strong picket lines. Thus, he said, "with the political power in their hands, the workers would quickly win this strike, or any other strike." In concluding, he reminded his hearers of the Socialist Party's aim: to abolish capitalism. "Although the Socialist Party is ready and willing to use its power to help the workers win the battles of the present," he said, "its ultimate aim is a revolution which will sweep out of existence the cause of strikes."

The thousands gathered in the park roared their approval. As the *Plain Dealer* was forced to admit the day after the rally, "Judged by the reception tendered each, Ruthenberg will be Cleveland's next Mayor."

On September 11, as stated in *The Women's Garment Workers,* the ranks of the strikers were still solid. Of three thousand workers who voted on whether to continue the strike, only 124 wanted to quit. The strikers received, furthermore, wide popular support. The president of the Ohio State Suffrage League, Mrs. Harriet Upton Taylor, for example, along with Toledo's liberal Mayor Brand Whitlock, spoke at strikers' mass meetings. But the police, the imported strikebreakers, thugs and provacateurs, and the vicious anti-labor tyranny of the Cloak Manufacturers' Association, who refused every offer of mediation, finally broke the strike. The gun thugs on the outside were helped by company-paid spies sent into the workers' ranks. The *Citizen* exposed a company "guard" named Patterson, whom the police had inadvertently arrested on the charge of carrying concealed weapons, as a professional strikebreaker in the employ of the Woodward Detective Agency of Pittsburgh. The International finally called off the strike, late in October. Even then, it was said that only eight hundred were in favor of returning to work. The strikers went back to their jobs without winning a single one of their demands.

In addition to these specific campaigns, Ruthenberg lived the more-than-full life of a party propagandist and organizer. He was put on the committee for local legislation, and on the State Executive Committee. He was a delegate to the State Socialist Convention in Columbus at the beginning of May. He was an unsuccessful candidate for delegate to the State Constitutional Convention which in 1912 was to amend Ohio's 140-year-old Constitution, and was chairman of the Party committee to propose amendments to that Constitution. He addressed several meetings—indoor and outdoor—every week. On May Day, 1911,

Ruthenberg had been the main speaker on Public Square to a crowd of more than six thousand people in a celebration described by the *Citizen* as the "largest ever held in Cleveland." Afterward, four thousand carrying red flags paraded to Acme Hall, with several bands playing the Marseillaise. And there, Cleveland's two Socialist Sunday Schools provided entertainment.

Socialist Sunday Schools were organized for the purpose of giving workers' children some elementary understanding of what the working class was fighting for. The first Cleveland Sunday School was set up in 1910. Such literature as Nicholas Klein's *Socialist Primer,* a first reader with pictures by cartoonist Ryan Walker, and the *Little Socialist Magazine,* described as the "leading monthly for boys and girls," were used as texts.

Lecturing and Learning

Ruthenberg's favorite lecture topic this year was "Scientific Socialism," into which he put the cream of his reading of Marx and Engels. For the Young People's Socialist League, in which he took a great interest, he talked on "Parliamentary Law" at a meeting on May 25, in Socialist Hall. A Hungarian woman of Cleveland remembers how as a child she used to pass the hat for Socialist contributions when Ruthenberg spoke at the Hungarian Workers' Hall, 4309 Lorain Avenue. Her mother, she says, "wanted us children to hear him," and she never forgot the impression he made. "His name always drew a crowd," she recalls. "The Hungarian people are very hard to approach if one is formal. Ruthenberg was very plain and friendly. And when he got through, he never got off the platform and just went away. He'd go among the workers and greet them."

On the State Executive Committee, Ruthenberg closely scrutinized every proposal before approving or rejecting. When the local in Salem, Ohio, asked for approval of its newly adopted municipal program, it was Ruthenberg who drily moved its rejection because, as the September *Bulletin* reported, it contained no statement of the "fundamental principle of the Socialist Party—the abolition of private ownership of the means of production and distribution and the substitution of collective ownership and democratic management." Numerous inner-party problems had to be settled. The Ohio party, groping its way to some understanding of the Negro question, began to understand the special position of the Negro in America. Resolution No. 9, adopted by the May Convention, recognized that the Negro "holds a peculiar position in society." The Convention invited Negroes to join the Socialist Party and urged the State Executive Committee to engage "competent speakers" for Negro audiences. In the July *Ohio Socialist Bulletin* a local appealed for "some colored comrade" as a speaker for the town's Negro population. As far as segregated locals for women were concerned, the September *Bulletin* carried the State Executive Committee's answer to Local Hamilton County, "We do not favor separate organization of women," but explained that women's committees should be set up in every local.

In the meantime, two persons died whose lives had influenced Ruthenberg. Robert Bandlow, whose letters in 1908 had drawn Ruthenberg toward the Socialist Party, died January 29, 1911.[3] Bandlow was a member of the Socialist party's National Committee, had once been a leader in the old Knights of Labor, and —as organizer of Typographia No. 6—held an important position in the AFL. His association with Bandlow gave Ruthenberg a close-up view of that oldstyle Socialist top leadership which he was shortly to challenge. Tom Johnson died April 10.[4] Though Ruthenberg had outgrown his youthful enthusiasm for the reform Mayor, he respected the man's accomplishments. A statue of Johnson was erected on Public Square, "located"—as the inscription says—"on the spot he dedicated to the freedom of speech." It was at the foot of this statue that Ruthenberg was to make some of his most historic speeches.

While Ruthenberg did not become Mayor of Cleveland, some fifteen smaller Ohio towns elected Socialist mayors in 1911. Indeed, *before* November, 1911, Ohio was listed as the *twenty-second* state in number of Socialists elected to office, but *after* that date it was *second*.[5] In other states several Socialists got into office, but the showing made by Ohio this year (and for several years thereafter) was outstanding. This success meant, however, a new series of problems to which Socialist leaders—

and especially Ruthenberg—were obliged to give thought. It is worth noting here that the Socialist Party carried on much local work in the towns where it won election victories, especially in connection with issues affecting workers, such as health, housing, and schools. Nowhere was this practical Socialist achievement more conspicuous than in Ohio.

The unusual electoral showing must be credited in part to Ruthenberg's aggressive, astute political activity, and in some part, too, to Ohio's generally progressive traditions. But there was also a solid economic base for this upsurge in Socialist thinking. Ohio had become a state in 1803, and thus was one of the oldest states in the union except for the original thirteen. Its industries—and its working class—were well established. Cleveland's railroad docks on Lake Erie (where Ruthenberg's father had toiled) were able to service the largest of lake boats and had been built in 1878. Ohio's total "tangible wealth" in 1910 was more than five billion dollars, and this increased to nine billion in 1912. Ohio ranked fourth among the states in population in 1910, and its great industrial towns were peopled with a militant proletariat. There were more than half a million wage-earners—largely in coal, steel, shipping—in Ohio in 1914.[6]

One of the hugest monopoly combines in the world, the Rockefeller empire, had its start with the forming of the Standard Oil Company of Ohio, which, by 1911, had off-shoots in many other states. It was in 1911 that the United States Supreme Court "dissolved" one of these off-shoots, the Standard Oil Company of New Jersey.[7] Rockefeller money was one of the dominant factors in industry all over the country, as, for instance, in the Colorado Fuel and Iron Company. As a part of the grab-and-exploit campaign of Big Business, an employers' anti-union offensive, which had started in Dayton, Ohio, in 1900 with the forming of a "citizens' alliance" of thirty-eight firms, spread for the next ten years or more. By 1906 the "soulless corporation" of United States Steel was open shop in all its plants, and by 1908 the Lake Carriers Association ("The Vassal of Steel") was also open shop, with a blacklist.[8]

Labor fought back, and the fight-back spirit was reflected not only in unionization but in the Socialist vote. A culmination of the great labor struggles of the period (going a little beyond this chapter) was the Youngstown, Ohio, strike at the Republic Iron and Steel Company in 1915-16.[9] The United Mine Workers, with a considerable membership in Ohio, tripled its size from 1900 to 1913.[10] The struggles nationally forced the setting up of a congressional Commission on Industrial Relations in 1912 which held extended hearings and issued a monumental report on the "underlying causes for dissatisfaction in the industrial situation." This unprecedented governmental report, signed by the nationally known liberal lawyer Frank P. Walsh as chairman and Basil M. Manly as director of research, revealed that the "basic cause" of workers' discontent was "low wages," and that industrial violence could be laid at the door of the employers because of their efforts to put strikebreakers into workers' jobs.[11]

Throughout Ohio, the election month of November, 1911, brought 1,353 new members into the party, making a new high total of 10,802. Ohio was now the third state in the Union in number of Socialists, exceeded only by New York and Pennsylvania. Largest Ohio locals were Cleveland and Columbus; in March, Local Columbus passed Local Cleveland in membership, boasting 1,089 members to Cleveland's 1,072, but by September Cleveland was again in the lead, with 1,608 members as against 1,447 in Columbus. While Ruthenberg was campaigning for mayor, Cleveland increased its membership more than 50 per cent. Local Cincinnati, which used to be the largest, had been left far behind.

A grave international development in 1911 compelled Ruthenberg to give serious thought to the war danger implicit in modern capitalism, and to the duty of the working class in forestalling that danger. War threatened with Mexico, on the most brazen imperialist excuse. On March 7, 1911, Republican President William Howard Taft ordered American troops to the Mexican border and sent American warships to Mexican ports in both oceans. The announced purpose was to prevent smuggling of arms to the Mexican insurgents struggling to overthrow the tyrant, Porfirio Diaz. The real purpose was to protect American investments in Mexico, which meant protecting the corrupt Diaz government. American money interests had found Diaz a willing tool.

The Socialist Party's National Executive Committee issued a proclamation, "Withdraw the Troops." The proclamation said Diaz had "destroyed the freedom of suffrage, speech, press and assembly," and had "exiled, imprisoned and assassinated" many patriots who sought to restore popular rule. Socialist Ohio's May Convention said in Resolution No. 1, "We declare our unity with our Mexican comrades and fellow workers in their struggle, with all financial and moral support within our power." The Taft administration's threat of war against Mexico did not materialize at this time, but five years later, under Wilson's administration (we shall have occasion to mention this again), United States troops did commit aggression against our southern neighbor.

"The Deep Desire in Every Man"

In odd moments Ruthenberg undertook to answer certain persistent arguments against socialism that every propagandist had to meet.

One of these was the assertion that Socialists are only "dreamers," indulging in fantasy far removed from reality. In the *Citizen,* February 11, he turned the tables by charging socialism's opponents themselves with dreaming. Quoting the maxim, "Nothing is permanent but change," he wrote: "Who are the dreamers? The Socialists, who say that society will continue to evolve and that social production existing today must lead to social distribution; or the capitalists, who say, 'We are reaping the rewards. Sun, stand still!' "

Another objection that Socialist speakers ran into was the accusation that Socialists believe in "free love." "Socialism as a political principle," he wrote, "has nothing to do with free love. If there are any changes in the marriage relation in the future, they will . . . be decreed by the social conscience of the human race, and we can rest assured that, just as the changes which have come in the past have improved and placed the sexual relations on a higher plane, so these changes of the future will tend to make these relations more ideal."

A third argument offered by enemies of socialism—that "socialism would kill incentive"—was tackled by Ruthenberg in the *Citizen* of May 2. "This objection," he wrote, "carries with it the suggestion that under capitalism there is an incentive for every one to live such a life as is of the most benefit to society as a whole."

But what is this heavenly incentive? Ruthenberg presented it as follows: "The capitalist system says in effect to every individual: The world is before you. . . . If you are strong, if you are crafty, if you are ready to crush out of your heart any sense of justice, of honesty, of helpfulness for the weak and unfortunate, you may take all that you desire. You may grind your fellow men under foot. . . . Capitalism judges ability and success by profits produced only, and offers no reward to the humane or altruistic employer. . . . The motive force of capitalism is greed. To the wage-worker capitalism offers as an incentive either a life of drudgery, at wages which scarcely enable him to provide an existence for himself and family, or one chance in a hundred thousand or so (the chances are decreasing as our industries concentrate) that he may climb on the backs of his fellow-workers to drive them to greater efforts. If a workingman possesses those qualities which capitalism rewards—selfishness, arrogance, egoism, if he can keep himself free from all other-regarding qualities—then he may be set over his fellow-workmen to drive them to greater efforts. But his work will always be judged by the profits he produces. He must not determine his action by deciding whether they are right, fair, just, but by whether this or that action will produce *more profits.*"

Against the "incentive" of capitalism Ruthenberg posed that of socialism, which would "give to all the opportunity of living happy, healthy lives." He concluded, characteristically, *"Socialism will appeal to . . . the deep desire in every man and woman to be of some service to mankind.*

4

LEFT SPOKESMAN

THE SCENE was Tomlinson Hall, Indianapolis, where the 1912 presidential nominating convention of the Socialist Party was taking place. Visitors crowded the balconies and swarmed through the corridors, pushing against the roped-in enclosure where the delegates' tables were. The delegates themselves, 277 of them, huddled and muttered in impromptu state caucuses. Many of them were angry and puzzled. The convention was more than half over—there would be only two more days—and not a single major issue had yet come up on the floor.

James F. Carey, Massachusetts state secretary, first Socialist Assemblyman to be elected in that state, and Right-wing leader, was in the chair. Beside him sat the vice-chairman for the day, May Wood Simons of Kansas, writer and lecturer and wife of A. M. Simons. The chair had just announced "debate" on the report of the Committee on Farmers' Program. The report, a typical Populist document advocating such reforms as government ownership of storage and transportation facilities and the setting up of agricultural experiment stations, was drawn up by a committee headed by A. M. Simons of Kansas, a historian, and including Oscar Ameringer of Oklahoma, editor of *The American Guardian,* Carl D. Thompson of Wisconsin, head of the Public Ownership League, and Algernon Lee of New York, head of the Rand School of Social Science—Right-wingers all.

Some half-dozen suggested amendments had already been "laid on the table," when Delegate Tom Clifford of Ohio roared out: "I want to know if the policy is to be pursued by the Chairman to cut off debate on every section of this report that is offered." He was promptly ruled "out of order."

Delegate Ruthenberg of Ohio asked for the floor. This was

his first national convention, and this was the first time he had addressed the assemblage. "I move the adoption of a new section, Number 10, to read as follow," he said, as the delegates leaned forward to listen: "We also point out that the above should be considered only as an immediate program, and that we demand the ultimate collective ownership of all the land used for productive purposes."[1]

Again the Right steam roller, which had been operating steadily for four days, got under way with a motion to lay this Socialist proposal on the table. But Ruthenberg was not to be downed so easily. "As maker of the motion," he insisted, his tall figure holding up the steam roller for a moment, "I have the right to the floor even if the motion to lay on the table is made."

Chairman Carey was taken aback. "Will you point out where that appears in the rules?" he asked in some confusion. Right-winger John Spargo of Vermont, Socialist author and lecturer, helped out the chair by inquiring how much time was left for debate. Spargo some years later became a Coolidge Republican and a propagandist for the utility companies. "Two minutes," Carey said, and ruled, "Comrade Ruthenberg's point is not well taken." Ruthenberg appealed from the decision of the chair. A voice vote was taken, and it was ruled that the chair was sustained.

But the Left was not satisfied. The Convention had adopted Roberts' *Rules of Order*. Ruthenberg sarcastically exlaimed: "Under Roberts' *Rules of Order* the right of the delegate to state his position has been denied him!" Ohio delegates Lawrence A. Zitt and William Bessemer insisted that Ruthenberg should be given the floor. In the midst of the confusion, the chair hurriedly put the question on the Farm Committee's report, and declared it adopted.

Delegate Lewis J. Duncan of Montana, mayor of Butte, shouted, "We have had about enough of this steam roller business this morning," and added: "We are working under Roberts' *Rules of Order* and for that reason I think for the information of this convention we should hear that rule read, and the attempt of the chair to keep us from having the rule read does not look good to me."

Again the chair was appealed from, and this time a show of hands was demanded. Eighty-six delegates—a minority, but a big minority—raised their hands in opposition to the chair. "In the name of those 86 noes I demand a roll call," shouted Zitt of Ohio. Even George Goebel of New Jersey began to think the rule should be read, and said so, but Morris Hillquit of New York was against it. "No discussion is in order," he rasped out, in a steely voice, "nothing except the roll call."

The Left won a small victory. The Secretary was forced to read the rule Ruthenberg had referred to, Section 54 of Paragraph 19, indicating that the introducer of a resolution "should always claim the floor to which he is entitled." The rule was clear, but it was a foregone conclusion that the chair would be sustained, rule or no rule. The 86 noes, however, swelled to 93 in the roll call, with 167 votes backing up the steam rolling chairman.

The forcing of the roll call at this juncture was significant and historic. This was the first of only four roll calls taken during the entire convention. The second, on the notorious "Sabotage Clause" of the Party Constitution (about which more later), was to come out almost the same, with 90 Left votes against the clause, and 191 from the Right favoring it. The same delegates, almost to a man, who supported Ruthenberg in the first roll call also opposed the "Sabotage Clause" in the second. The other roll calls were on nominations of candidates for president and vice-president, respectively.

Leading the Right line-up were the two master wire-pullers, Hillquit and Berger. Hillquit, a New York lawyer, and indeed the recognized leader of the Party, was the smooth faction-tactician; Berger, elected Socialist Congressman from Wisconsin in 1911, was the successful vote-getter. And who was on the Left? Only unknown or little-known men, like Ruthenberg himself, chiefly Ohio delegates and those from the Northwest, with a few representatives from Michigan, Pennsylvania and other states. (William D. Haywood was present as a member of the National Executive Committee, but was not a delegate.) These persistent rank-and-filers, doggedly voting for a working class position in these roll calls, represented the new and growing force in the

Socialist Party. The roll calls revealed the historic cleavage between Right and Left that had developed in the party. Ruthenberg, as he rose up in Tomlinson Hall that morning of May 16, challenging the Right steam roller, was stepping forward for the first time as a national spokesman of the Left.

Reforms and Reformism

The conflict between Right and Left in 1912 centered around the party attitude toward the trade unions and toward reforms. Yet at bottom the conflict was deeper than its ideological expression. It was a conflict between working class consciousness and middle class opportunism. The Socialist Party was not only not united—it was not homogeneous in members' ideas of what Socialism meant. The Populist-reformist way of thinking was still there (which sought not to abolish capitalism but to modify it or muzzle it) plus a hang-over of DeLeonist sectarianism (which held aloof from practical mass struggles and, in the words of William Z. Foster, "propagated socialism in the abstract"). This non-working class, non-Marxist element took over control. The advanced proletarian elements were neither sufficiently developed in theory nor strong enough in numbers to hold the leadership of their own party.

Haywood, only Left member of the party's seven-man National Executive Committee and head of the Industrial Workers of the World, was the leading exponent of a part of correct trade union theory—that of organization by industry rather than craft. But this excellent segment of theory was made ineffective by its anarcho-syndicalist base and by the setting up of dual unions and the consequent dividing of organized labor.

Ruthenberg did not meet William Z. Foster, the man who was to develop American trade union theory much further, until 1921, but their paths intertwined more or less before that date. While Ruthenberg, in Cleveland, was joining the Socialist Party in 1909, Foster, in Seattle, was being forced out of it in a Left versus Right intra-party battle. In 1911, after two years' experience as a member of the IWW, Foster was already dissatisfied with the dual unionism practiced by that organization.

As he explained in *From Bryan to Stalin,* he came back from Europe in September, 1911, and "took up the question of winning the IWW for a policy of boring-from-within" the AFL, and had talks with Haywood on the question. Ruthenberg read in the *Citizen,* December 30, 1911, Foster's quoted remark that "there is no place in organized labor for two organizations, but . . . for the common interests of all it would be better to have one organization, even if that organization is not all that is to be desired."[2] In 1912, while Ruthenberg was concerned with the Socialist Party's national convention, Foster was organizing the Syndicalist League of North America, with a program which aimed at any cost to avoid the IWW mistake of building new trade unions in fields already unionized, but sought persistently to convince AFL trade unionists that industrial unionism was the thing to work for. Foster's abstention from the Socialist Party after 1909—his "greatest political mistake," as he later wrote in his *History of the Communist Party of the United States*—kept him and Ruthenberg separated until the great Communist reorganizing year of 1921.

Ruthenberg was not himself a union member. He was a white-collar worker, and there were no white-collar unions in those days. He had had no direct trade union experience. But he was close to the workers of Cleveland in their daily struggles, and he remembered clearly—and with great understanding now—the proletarian viewpoint of his father. In all his thinking he passionately identified himself with the working class.

The split over reforms, or "immediate demands," centered around the Left's opposition to reformism, mere office seeking and all-round opportunism. Some of the Left, notably the delegation from Washington State, were so embittered by the frequent substitution of reformism for Socialism in the party propaganda that they mistook all reforms, even those most necessary for the working class, for *reformism.* Forgetting the *Communism Manifesto's* teaching about "enforcement of the momentary interests of the working class," the Washington delegates demanded that all immediate demands be taken out of the Socialist platform, which they said should contain nothing but the demand for socialism. Even some of the Ohio delegates supported the Washington position. Ruthenberg showed his more balanced attitude on immediate demands when he challenged the Right on the farm question, as described earlier. He did not suggest that reforms be left out of the party's farm program, but neither was he going to let socialist aims be left out of it.

The collision on industrial unionism and on reformism at the 1912 Socialist Convention hastened the crystallization of Left and Right trends into Left and Right wings. This schism resulted only later in a party split; but the 1912 Convention revealed clearly the open and recognized division within the party which was to lead to the real split of 1919. The emergence of the Left was in a sense forecast by a resolution brought to the Convention by the Ohio delegation, with the exception of Max S. Hayes and the Reverend F. C. Strickland. The resolution charged the party "with becoming conservative," as the official *Proceedings,* edited by John Spargo, gingerly recorded.[3] The Right steam roller turned the statement over to the Right Resolutions Committee, which promptly buried it.

While sharing many of the weaknesses of the Left, Ruthenberg approached labor's problems from a broad and thoughtful viewpoint. He avoided anarchist pitfalls, always basing himself on political action, and fought tenaciously against dividing the labor front, insisting that capitalism was the main enemy and that labor could solve its internal disagreement by discussion and argument. However, the Left wing in which he participated was permeated, Foster has shown, by dual union sentiment.[4] Ruthenberg lined up with the Left in every inner-party struggle, but he remained in the party until the final split over imperialist war and other policies in the 1917-1919 years. In 1912, and during the five years that followed, Ruthenberg was thinking toward a correct application of Marxism to the United States. His merit was that he combined a sober search for a correct Marxist tactic with steady organizational activity. He was able to mobilize the Left within the Socialist Party when the time came.

Ruthenberg was handicapped in theoretical development by lack of leisure to read and reflect, and, especially, by the low

Marxist level of the Socialist Party which provided no incentive to discussion even of the most immediately crucial questions. The American Socialist Party leadership kept aloof from the theoretical and political polemics that developed in the Socialist parties of Europe. This lack of intellectual ferment was not conducive to the political growth of the Socialist Left.[5] A few years after, to be sure, when the writings of Lenin became available in English, and the Communist movement got under way, there was a tremendous acceleration of theoretical development in American working class circles.

Industrial Unionism

Most delegates expected an open break between Right and Left when the Resolution on "Labor Organizations and Their Relation to the Party" was presented on the fifth afternoon. The nine-man Committee on Labor Organizations had three Left-minded members: Tom Clifford of Ohio, Tom Hickey of Texas, and Tom J. Lewis of Oregon. The "three Toms" were expected to bring in a minority report, and the Left to fight to get it adopted. Agreement of Right and Left on a single resolution was—everyone thought—impossible. When the impossible happened, and a single resolution was offered on the afternoon of May 16, a great gain seemed to have been achieved. Right-winger Oscar Ameringer, member of the Farm Committee whose report Ruthenberg had tried to get amended that morning, was chairman of the Labor Committee. He was supported by other Right colleagues, notably Algernon Lee of New York, who at the 1910 Congress had advocated exclusion of Oriental immigrants,[6] and Job Harriman of California.

Despite everything, a resolution was drawn up which had some good features, and the Left accepted it as the best that could be achieved. The resolution praised the "amalgamation of related trades into federations and industrial unions," a concession to the industrial unionists. It denounced the "demoralizing politics represented by the National Civic Federation," a slap at the AFL, two of whose leaders, Samuel Gompers and Matthew Woll, were serving on the anti-labor Civic Federation's board (even after John Mitchell of the United Mine Workers had resigned from it the year before at the insistence of his union). The resolution called on all unions to undertake the "task of organizing the unorganized, especially the immigrants and the unskilled laborers," thus emphasizing a problem the IWW had tried to solve and the AFL had neglected; and it urged organized labor to welcome new recruits by "abolishing all onerous conditions of membership," a crack at the AFL's exorbitant initiation fees. But the resolution said that only workers on the job could "solve the problems of form of organization," and reaffirmed the Socialist Party's neutrality on "questions of form of organization or technical methods of action in the industrial struggle." Thus the party praised industrial unionism, but refrained from telling how to get it. As in 1908, it failed to give theoretical guidance.

The Left looked upon this compromise as a victory. "Astonishment showed on every face," the *International Socialist Review* said, in reporting the proceedings in its June number, "and then followed a tumultuous yell as the Convention woke up to the fact that a bitter fight had been averted." The official *Proceedings* records that at this point there were cries of "Haywood," and Haywood, given the floor, declared it his belief that the labor resolution should be adopted. The IWW leader, though not a delegate, was—says cartoonist Art Young in his autobiography—the dominating figure at the gathering.[7] The Right feared him. "To my mind this is the greatest step that has ever been taken by the Socialist Party of America," he said. Reminding the delegates that he had always urged every worker to join a union and to use a ballot if he had one, Haywood concluded, "So, as Tom Hickey has shaken hands with Job Harriman for the first time in twenty years, I feel that I can shake hands with every delegate in this convention and say that we are a united working class." The Labor Committee's resolution was adopted, and the whole auditorium heaved a sigh of relief.

How, then, was the division brought into the open? The cleavage between Right and Left was recorded historically by a vote on an entirely different matter: *alleged advocacy of sabotage!* The Right-wingers engineered it the very next morning, by bringing up the scarecrow of "direct action" to stampede the delegates.

The Sabotage Clause

"You will have a split yet, and I am ready to split right now!" So said Victor Berger the next day, in the discussion on the Sabotage Clause brought up as an amendment to the party's constitution.[8]

Morris Hillquit was chairman of the Constitution Committee, on which there were no Ohio delegates. Ruthenberg had been nominated to this Committee, but was crowded off. This was one committee where the Executive wanted no minority report. There were no Left members. Ruthenberg was an expert on constitutions. He had been chairman of the committee that revised the Ohio Socialist Party constitution, and chairman of the party committee to make proposals to the Ohio State Constitutional Convention. Sitting at the table with the other Ohio delegates, he had watched for five days the maneuvering of the Right-wing, and when the "sabotage" matter came up, his face was grim. He didn't believe in sabotage, but who did? Was an imaginary danger to be formally denounced in order to slow down militant class struggle? Was that the design of the Right?

The overwhelming majority of the Socialist Party, both Left and Right, opposed the anarcho-syndicalist bombast that was creeping into IWW theory. The Left, while opposing the so-called "direct action" propaganda, discounted its importance; but they felt sympathy and admiration for the IWW's steadfast fight for industrial unionism and its heroic strike struggles against police and employer violence. The Right, on the other hand, tended to exaggerate the growth of syndicalist thinking in the American labor and socialist movement. They had been disturbed the year before by the appearance of the pamphlet, *Industrial Socialism,* by Wm. D. Haywood and Frank Bohn. The latter was a free-lance writer and a former Socialist Labor Party secretary. Both authors were editors of the *International Socialist Review,* and Haywood was on the Party's executive committee. The pamphlet never once mentioned "direct action" or "sabotage," but it did contain some flamboyant phraseology that suggested methods associated with these terms. The pamphlet said that the industrial worker "retains absolutely no respect for the property 'rights' of the profit-takers. He will use any weapon which will win his fight."[9] The Right, studying this passage, suspected that forms of strike violence might eventually be sponsored in the U.S.—in the name of socialism. They were determined to nip any such possibility in the bud.

It is interesting at this point, in view of Ruthenberg's closeness to Debs in those years, to note how Debs viewed the controversial passage from Haywood and Bohn referred to above. In a letter to a friend, March 5, 1913, Debs said that he too would use any weapon that would help win a strike, and that he too had no respect for capitalist laws. "But," he added, "this does not imply that I propose making an individual law-breaker of myself and butting my head against the stone wall of existing property laws." Furthermore, he went on, "for the same reason I am opposed to sabotage and to 'direct action.'"[10] Ruthenberg's ideas, and the Left's generally, were much the same. The Left realized the need for struggle, but took sober account of actual conditions and possibilities.

Curiously enough, the word *sabotage* was not in Article II, Section 6, as Hillquit first read it to the assemblage. The Committee's original clause denounced "crime against the person or other methods of violence." A Missouri delegate named W. L. Carver rose, as though prompted, to substitute "sabotage" for "against the person," so that the clause would read: "Any member of the party who opposes political action or advocates crime, sabotage, or other methods of violence as a weapon of the working class to aid in its emancipation shall be expelled from membership in the party."

Members of the Committee leaped to support the Sabotage amendment, including Chairman Hillquit himself, who had just declared that his Committee was unanimous on the first version. First to plug for the word *sabotage* was the Rev. W. R. Gaylord of Wisconsin, who declared that "crime against property is a thing that this party cannot stand for." To make his own class position clear, Gaylord said that he stood "for the maintaining of the social order which we have, and under which we live." The storm of opposition was a veritable demonstration. The way in which the introduction of the word *sabotage* had been staged was not lost on the Left. "Now," said Clifford of Ohio, "we dropped these things yesterday for the sake of peace and harmony, and today someone has injected that section into this Constitution for a purpose." Hickey of Texas shouted, "Why? . . . Peanut politics, that is what it is."

Dan Hogan of Arkansas wanted the whole crime-sabotage-violence clause struck out. The Socialist Party, he said, "has never been a party of violence. It has never been accused of any such thing by those who were acquainted with its history. There is no reason why we should blazon forth to the world that we stand against a thing when there was never a suspicion among ourselves or among those who knew us that we stood for it. . . . Now if we are going to put the whole moral code in the Constitution, then I ask you to be equally consistent and put in a specific declaration against larceny, put in a specific declaration against polygamy, put in a specific declaration against free love. . . . We don't need to tell people that we stand for law and order." Marguerite Prevey of Ohio pointed to the danger this clause would constitute in the hands of reactionary courts. "Now," she said, "the capitalist class are interpreting the laws so that in every strike where there is any property destroyed, the working men who are out on strike may be indicted for being accessories before the fact and be jailed, when they had no part in destroying this property. . . . If we adopt this clause . . . are we, the Socialist Party, going to expel from the party a workingman convicted by the capitalist courts of destroying property?" Delegate J. O. Bentall, one of the few Left-wingers from Illinois, put his finger on the real source of the cleavage between Right and Left. "There is an element in the Socialist Party today," he said, "that is progressive and wants to go forward . . . and there is another element that stands conservative, reactionary, monkeying with the old, outworn machinery. There is the division . . . and not sabotage or violence or anything of the kind."

Right-wingers, in replying to these statements, did not confine themselves to logical argument. Victor Berger excelled in invective, attacking everyone not of the Right as an anarchist. He even slandered the Haymarket martyrs of 1886. He sneered at the current San Diego free speech fighters and, by implication, supported the frame-up charge of murder then being pressed against two IWW leaders of the Lawrence strike, Joseph Ettor and Arturo Giovannitti.

"I want to say to you, comrades," Berger cried, "that I for one do not believe in murder as a means of propaganda; I do not believe in theft as a means of expropriation; nor in a continuous riot as a free speech agitation." And, wrote Haywood afterward in his autobiography, "he knew that at the time he was speaking Ettor, Giovannitti and Caruso [leaders in the New England textile strike of 1912] were in prison charged with murder[11] It was no credit to Berger that they were later acquitted. Upon his implied reference to the Lawrence strike leaders, the Left called out for Haywood, but he was not given the floor.

Hillquit, as chairman of the Constitution Committee, had the last word. Stating that his Committee "unanimously" (with one dissenting) accepted the insertion of the word *sabotage,* he proceeded to becloud the issue by substituting a different proposition for the one the delegates were voting on. He made it appear that the vote was to express approval or disapproval of sabotage. All who dared vote against the Sabotage Clause, he hinted, might "perhaps be suspected of a fondness" for sabotage itself.

Then came the roll call on the question, Shall the Sabotage Clause be struck out? Midst tense quiet, the secretary droned out the 277 names. Among the 90 of the Left who had the courage to make a stand, C. E. Ruthenberg spoke out clearly—"Yes." Right Socialist leaders in 1912 simply took over the anti-IWW journalistic slanders of the time and gave them authenticity against the whole labor movement. It was like turning state's evidence against the most active strike leaders in the country. Against the background of the events of those days, this was the actual significance of Article II, Section 6, adopted by the Convention as an amendment to the Socialist Party constitution.

Meanwhile, telegrams were coming to the Convention calling for aid to the IWW-led free speech fight then going on in San Diego. The messages were referred to the Right-controlled National Executive Committee, which shamelessly delayed action on them. On the morning of May 15, Left delegates demanded that protests be made to the Governor of California on behalf of the free speech fighters, whose leaders were threatened with kidnapping and violence. Haywood asked to make a statement, but was denied the floor. Spargo and Job Harriman insisted on further deliberation by the NEC. Late that afternoon, the NEC got around to its San Diego proposals, which included a contribution of $250; a message to Governor Hiram Johnson of California in which he was "'urged" to make public the results of his own investigation of the facts; and a telegram to AFL organizations of California, offering to cooperate with them.

But why not also "cooperate" with the San Diego IWW, which was leading the fight, demanded Kate Sadler of Washington and William Bessemer of Ohio. Right-wingers led by Harriman and Spargo (while Morris Hillquit and Victor Berger kept discreet silence) fought like troopers to prevent even mention of the IWW, in this message on a struggle which the IWW was leading. But the Sadler-Bessemer motion to include the IWW was finally carried.

Party Democracy

The cleavage between Right and Left revealed itself also in matters of party structure and party democracy. This was apparent on two occasions when Ruthenberg challenged the party's bureaucracy—first on the status of language organizations, and later on the composition of the new National Committee.

The Socialist Party at that time included in its membership a considerable number of foreign-speaking Federations, each having practically complete autonomy, with no organizational contact with the party except through translator-secretaries in the national office. This set-up held back the Americanization of immigrants in these groups and delayed the full assimilation of foreign-speaking Socialists into the Socialist Party. The report of the Committee on Foreign-Speaking Organizations, headed by Right-winger Lewis Goaziou of Pennsylvania, recommended continuation of this arrangement.

In proposing a change, Ruthenberg explained the situation in Cleveland, where some twenty language groups were in the party, yet—so far as the local was concerned—were *not* in the party. Members of these groups paid their dues to the National Office and "never came near" the city central organization, he complained. There was no cooperation between the language sections and the city local they were supposed to be affiliated with. If foreign-speaking Socialists were required to buy their dues stamps from the city central body just as English-speaking branches did, he argued, there would be a closer relationship and better cooperation down below. Ruthenberg's stand was so clearly correct that some language federation leaders whose ties were with the Right supported him. But Spargo and National Secretary J. Mahlon Barnes tried to make it appear that Ruthenberg objected altogether to organizing language groups, and his amendment was defeated.[12]

On the question of the composition of the National Committee Ruthenberg again led the attack of the Left forces. Dissatisfaction with the rule of the Hillquit-Berger clique had forced Hillquit, chairman of the Constitution Committee, to make some gesture toward democratizing the national officialdom. His fair-sounding proposal was that the State Secretaries be included as members of the National Committee.

The State Secretaries of the Socialist Party were not necessarily or even usually the best theoretical or political leaders. Often the real party leaders occupied non-paid posts in outstanding locals, as was the case with Ruthenberg himself. Ruthenberg opposed Hillquit's proposal, urging that members of the National Committee be elected directly, as provided by the old constitution, one from each state and territory and an additional one for each 3,000 or fraction thereof.[13] George Goebel of New Jersey spoke against Ruthenberg's plan, saying, "I beg you not to stand for this amendment, because if you do . . .

you are only going back to the time when every Tom, Dick and Harry could be elected to the National Committee." Ruthenberg's amendment lost in this case, too, as had the previous one. However, as a result of behind-the-scenes complaints and compromises, Hillquit's Committee was obliged to modify the new clause so that either the State Secretary "or such other person as the members of the party in the state shall elect by referendum vote" would represent each state on the Committee. This alteration was made the last day of the Convention, when Ruthenberg was vice-chairman. It was brought up, interestingly enough, during an appeal from the decision of the chair, when Ruthenberg, for the first and only time during the Convention, wielded the gavel a few moments.

The Nomination of Debs

"You will not howl me down!" Morris Hillquit shouted, his face livid with rage. It was the afternoon of May 17. The roll call nomination for a presidential candidate was about to be taken at the Convention. For a wonder, a Left delegate was in the chair—Lewis J. Duncan, Mayor of Butte, Montana. The Convention had ruled earlier that there were to be no nominating speeches. Hillquit—for a reason of his own—was trying to get around this ruling, but all over the hall delegates were declaring for Debs and calling out for the roll call. This made Hillquit mad.

Hillquit, Berger and other Right bureaucrats had plotted to prevent Debs from being the party's standard bearer. Incredible as it may seem now, looking back, there was in 1912 a conspiracy by the inner circle to nominate a Right wing presidential candidate, and if possible to keep Debs from being nominated at all.[14] It was Hillquit's purpose to make a nominating speech for the well-known magazine writer, Charles Edward Russell of New York. He was foiled by the ruling of Chairman Duncan and the shouts of delegates for Debs. Hillquit appealed from the ruling, but Duncan's decision was sustained.

Then Berger jumped up, in another attempt. "Before we vote we ought to know whether Comrade Debs will accept," he said insinuatingly. Debs himself was not at the Convention.

According to Alexander Trachtenberg's monograph on Debs, the lion-hearted agitator "never was sent as a delegate to a national or international convention, never was permitted to participate in the councils of the party to formulate policies and work out tactics. The leadership of the Socialist Party studiously avoided bringing Debs into the organization."[15]

But in this case the chair's ruling and the unmistakable spirit of the delegates made short work of the plot to prevent Debs' nomination. Replying to Berger, Chairman Duncan brusquely stated there was no doubt Debs would accept. The roll call was taken. Eugene Victor Debs, for the fourth successive time, was chosen Socialist candidate for President. The actual vote was: Debs, 165; Emil Seidel, mayor of Milwaukee, 56; Charles Edward Russell, 54.

Examination of that historic roll call vote reveals the solid Left kernel of Debs' support. Every Left-winger voted for Debs. It also reveals that the Right top leadership—Hillquit, Berger, Spargo, Algernon Lee, George Allan England, Job Harriman, Meyer London, Oscar Ameringer and the rest—voted against Debs.

The convention's last roll call, on nomination for the vice-presidency, showed almost the same Left-Right cleavage as did the roll call on the Sabotage Clause. In this case, there was lacking the immense popularity of a Debs to split the Right vote. It was on principle rather than on fame that Dan Hogan of Arkansas got 73 Left votes. The Left delegates remembered his speech against the Sabotage Clause, and his vote to strike it out. The Right lined up almost to a man in support of Mayor Emil Seidel of Milwaukee. Seidel got 159 votes, and the nomination; John W. Slayton of Pennsylvania got 24. Hogan's 73 votes represented the heart of the Convention's Left wing.

The 1912 Convention did not solve the pressing problems that faced American Socialists, but it revealed what some of them were. The Socialist Party had reached in this year its point of highest growth, with a membership of 113,371,[16] and the earnestness and enthusiasm of the Convention started the process of acquainting the militant Socialists with each other and gradually aligning them in a Left wing.

5

SPADE WORK IN CLEVELAND

Ruthenberg was far from daunted by Right wing domination of the Indianapolis Convention. Back in Cleveland, as candidate for governor of Ohio, he undertook a dramatic county-to-county, village-to-village campaign over the entire state in an effort to reach every voter with the message of socialism. The result was that Ohio that year rolled up a larger Socialist vote than any other state in the Union.

In the very midst of the electioneering he was forced out of the state leadership by an underhanded maneuver, of which more later. He was not daunted by that, either, but settled down to two hard years of steady organizing work.

The Campaign for Governor

The governorship campaign began with a picnic in Cleveland's Luna Park. "Annual Socialist Picnic at Luna Park, Tuesday, July 16th, 1912," read the advertisement, flanked by pictures of the chief speakers, Ruthenberg and Haywood, across the front page of the July 13 Cleveland *Socialist,* party-owned weekly founded by Ruthenberg the previous November. "Baseball, Races, Balloon Ascension," the ad said. "Come early and stay late." The Socialists, said Haywood, in his speech at the picnic, are accused of stirring up class hatred. "I for one plead guilty," he declared. "I want you to hate the capitalist system, and I want you to hate the capitalist class." It was the capitalists who were doing the killing, he went on, pointing to the 25,000 workers killed annually in industrial accidents. It was the capitalists who drove 60,000 women annually into prostitution, and millions of children into wage slavery. "Who takes more than he earns is a thief," Haywood said in his advice to workers, "and who takes less, without protest, is a willing slave."

Ruthenberg had been nominated in April, and was candidate for governor when he went in June to the party's National Convention. The same paper which announced the Luna Park picnic carried an endorsement of Ruthenberg for governor by Local 303 of the International Molders Union of North America. Ruthenberg's campaign brought his wife Rose into the party. Baby Dandy was now a school boy seven years old, almost big enough to attend Socialist Sunday School. From this time on, Rose was often in the triangle-shaped hall on the second floor of 737 Prospect Avenue, taking part in mailing bees to send out campaign literature. She was secretary of Local Cleveland's Woman's Committee.

Ruthenberg made a full-time job of campaigning for the governorship. He started out June 20, went from town to town, and spoke night after night. By the end of September he had covered three-quarters of the state, and as the Cleveland *Citizen* said, "when he finishes his trip at Cleveland, November 4, he will have talked in every county of the state, and reached one hundred twenty cities and towns."[1] He was released for the duration of the campaign by his employer, head of the Webster Building Company, who was a Socialist. Ruthenberg had left the Johns-Manville Roofing Company late in 1911, to work for the Webster concern as head of the estimate department.

A tale of Ruthenberg's stumping tour came in from Fostoria, a town with a Socialist mayor, and somehow got printed in the October 29 issue of the Cleveland *Press,* one of the city's three capitalist papers. "A workingman appeared at one of the principal street corners here the other night," the story said, "carrying a gasoline lamp and a megaphone under one arm and some boards and a long pole under the other. A hammer stuck out of his coat pocket, and some nails jingled inside. On his lapel he wore the small red button of the Socialist Party. In ten minutes he had rigged up a platform, attached the gasoline lamp to the pole, and lighted the burner. Then he picked up the megaphone and started off down the middle of Main Street, shouting again and again as he went: 'Hear Charles E. Ruthenberg of Cleveland, the Socialist candidate for Governor of Ohio, tonight at the corner of Main and Center Streets.' In the meantime Ruthenberg himself had arrived in town. Nobody had met him at the depot, and he had carried his own grip to the hotel. He ate supper alone, and then for half an hour sat in the office reading the evening papers. About seven o'clock the Socialist mayor of Fostoria, W. M. Ralston, and the Socialist Director of Public Service, A. B. Hollenbaugh, dropped in and made themselves acquainted with their gubernatorial nominee. 'This meeting tonight, Governor, has cost us exactly ten cents,' said Mayor Ralston. 'I spent a dime for some gasoline for the lamp; we had the boards for the speakers' stand, and the street corner is free.' "

As the story said, while the old parties were putting up thousands of dollars for chartered trains and brass bands in their campaigns, Ruthenberg was collecting from his audiences as he went along enough money to pay his hotel bills and get him to the next town.

At Martins Ferry, another little town with a Socialist administration, Ruthenberg spoke from an undertaker's hearse. "I told my audience I rather liked to speak from such a vehicle," he said afterwards, with a dry smile, "as I'm in the business of directing the funeral of the old parties." Ohio's "able candidate for governor, C. E. Ruthenberg," reported the *International Socialist Review* of December, 1912, "was on the road continuously from July 1 to election day, and we doubt if any other candidate can beat his record for number of successful meetings held."

Ruthenberg's vote for the governorship of Ohio in 1912 was 87,709, a little less than the 89,930 votes which Ohio gave Debs. Debs' vote nationally that year for president was 901,839—nearly a million out of a total popular vote of 14 million (women not voting), or about six and one-half per cent. Ohio cast the largest Socialist vote in 1912 of any state in the Union. Illinois was second with 78,679 votes for John Kennedy, candidate for governor, and New York third with 56,917 for her candidate for governor, Charles Edward Russell.[2] This was the year of Theodore Roosevelt's "Bull Moose" Progressive Party platform, the best part of it stolen from the Socialists. It is a tribute to Ruthenberg's political leadership in Ohio that T. R.'s demagogy made no inroads on the state's Socialist voters, as the election figures show. On the contrary, the Socialists gained over previous years. Ohio's 1912 presidential vote was divided as follows: Woodrow Wilson, 423,152; W. H. Taft, 277,066; T. R. Roosevelt, 229,327; and Debs, 89,930.

What was it, Ruthenberg asked, in an article on August 24 in the *Arm and Torch,* that Roosevelt offered the working class? "The promise of reform—to smooth away some of the sharp corners of the profit system—will not free us from the evils of capitalism," he wrote. "We will accept all the concessions made us. . . . Some of the concessions will strengthen us. . . . But before us lies our goal"—the goal of socialism. He took note of the particular reforms, long advocated by Socialists, that were listed in the Bull Moose platform: a compensation law, old age pensions, an eight-hour day, minimum wage laws and laws against child labor. All to the good, he agreed, but, he went on, "We want more than that: we want to cease to be industrial slaves; we want to be free."

Looking into the future, beyond reforms of the old system, he wrote: "In the new life, we will organize our productive forces so that we can supply the needs of all. . . . This will give us . . . ample time for recreation. . . Literature, music and art will be ours to enjoy. We will delve deep in the history of the past, and our research will wrench from nature her last secret."

Ruthenberg laid down at the start of the campaign one of the Left's main principles—that mere office-getting is not and must not be a primary aim of the party of the working class. In a programmatic statement, "The Political Situation in Ohio," he declared: "We . . . must remember that municipal victories will not solve the problems before us. We cannot solve the problem of poverty, child labor, the exploitation of the working class, through municipal victories. We must, therefore, keep before the workers the ultimate goal of our movement, the achievement of complete political and industrial power, and the abolition of the capitalist system."

Ohio had elected more Socialists to office than any other state, hence, he insisted, Socialist office-holders in Ohio had a special responsibility: to make good as Socialists. Sometimes, he warned, elected Socialists become turncoats. He cited as examples the mayors of Lima and Lorain, who, after election, deserted socialism and went over to the old parties. "Both these hold a lesson for us," he explained. ". . . neither had a fundamental grasp of the principles of socialism, and . . . neither was thoroughly impregnated with working class ideals." Despite his interest in election work, Ruthenberg emphasized over and over again that parliamentary and election activity was only part of the job of socialism. "The election of a mayor or any other . . . official is merely an incident in our work," he said on one occasion.[3] The ultimate goal, he always pointed out, was the setting up of a socialist society, with justice, freedom and plenty for all.

Organizer and Educator

The Left wing of the Socialist Party surpassed the Right—at least in Ohio—in organizational activity. This was shown in the contrasting membership records for 1912 and 1913 of Local Cleveland, under Left leadership, and Local Columbus, stronghold of the Right. Before the 1912 convention, the two locals had been neck and neck in every membership drive. In January, 1912, Local Columbus reported 1,788 dues paying members, and Local Cleveland reported 1,891. By January, 1913, the Columbus membership had dwindled to 942, while the Cleveland organization—adding a hundred or more every month—had reached a total of 2,771. By June, 1913, Local Columbus had shrunk further to 872 members, while Local Cleveland, where Ruthenberg had just become the full time organizer, had 2,950.

An example of Ruthenberg's organizing methods is his "Instructions to Precinct Workers," in the Cleveland *Socialist,*

August 17. In each precinct, Socialists were advised to set up an "acurate and complete card index of all the Socialist sympathizers" in the neighborhood, to enlarge this index by house-to-house canvassing, to visit them at least once a month, give them literature, sell them tickets for lectures and affairs, ask them for donations, sign them up as subscribers to the Cleveland *Socialist,* and invite them to meetings. "Do not make long visits," he suggested. "Take pains to be pleasant and friendly."

Ruthenberg had a warm, sympathetic nature underneath his reserve. Some who knew him in those days saw him only as a person of driving energy, so intent on building the movement as to be almost cold in day-to-day contacts. Perhaps they did not chance to observe incidents that revealed him otherwise; perhaps Ruthenberg's own shyness hid his warmer feelings. His news notes, "Gathered on the Road," sent back to the Cleveland *Socialist* from various points of his two-months campaign tour, show a friendly personality, and a dry mid-western sense of humor. Salem, Ohio, where there was another Socialist mayor, showed the "advantage of having a Socialist administration," he wrote. He was speaking on a street corner when a heavy shower started, and, he said, the crowd simply "adjourned to the Council Chamber and continued there."

In some towns the residents were too fearful to approach a Socialist. When he talked in Columbiana, the people stood across the street or halfway down the block, straining their ears while the speaker strained his voice. As Ruthenberg described the scene, "There were probably a hundred and fifty people within hearing distance, but coaxing, cajolery, even his [the chairman's] funny stories did not bring more than ten in the circle around the box." When Ruthenberg got up to speak, he tried a new tack: "I . . . began my talk in a whisper." There was an immediate rush toward the speakers' stand, and soon all the hundred and fifty were gathered around.

In Massilon, Ruthenberg met "General" Jacob S. Coxey, who a generation before, during the 1893-4 economic crisis, had led the famous "Coxey's Army" to Washington in the first "hunger march." Coxey had joined Local Massilon.

"The tremendous growth of the movement makes it necessary

that the campaign this year should be one largely of education," Ruthenberg wrote in his report for the State Executive Committee on "The Political Situation in Ohio." It was Marxist education that he meant. "There are more copies of *Value, Price and Profit* [Karl Marx] sold in Ohio than in any other state," observed the *International Socialist Review*, June, 1912. Ruthenberg took special pains to widen the people's understanding of Marxist theory. In his lecture on "Scientific Socialism," given often in 1912, he explained the concepts of the class struggle, surplus value and dialectical materialism.

Socialism was a glorious future to look forward to, he explained, but it had to be fought for. "It is a happy omen," he editorialized in the Cleveland *Socialist*, commenting on the hearings before the Congressional Commission on Industrial Relations (which in the fall and winter of 1912-13 began to be widely discussed in the press), "that the spirit of revolt has grown so strong. . . . In this revolt lies the hope of the future."

Ruthenberg discussed the inevitability of socialism in an article entitled, "The Basis of Our Confidence," in the New York *Call*, Socialist daily paper, June 16. "We cannot turn back the hand of time," he wrote. "We must go forward. . . . The same process which has brought into existence the present situation [of industrial achievement] has developed the intellectual powers of the working class. It has placed them in a position which makes future progress and the birth of a new society, based upon new ideas of justice and equality, dependent upon *them*, and given them knowledge to use their power. We Socialists have faith in the working class. We believe the workers have advanced too far to submit to industrial slavery, and therefore our confidence that they will assert their power to bring into existence . . . the social ownership of the already socialized means of production."

Having established the Cleveland *Socialist*, Ruthenberg strove to set up a state-wide paper, to be called the Ohio *Socialist*. On his motion, at the State Socialist Convention in April, a Committee on Printing Plant was chosen. There was much talk but nothing was done. In September, as a member of the State Executive Committee, he urged: "That we make the consideration of the Ohio *Socialist* and printing plant the *first* order of business." He was made chairman of a sub-committee to carry out the plan. Then he ran into trouble.

Right and Left in Ohio

The State Executive Committee which supported Ruthenberg's proposal was overwhelmingly Left. The larger and more authoritative State Committee, however, was controlled by the Right. Right-wingers in Locals Dayton and Columbus launched an attack on the SEC, charging that its members were "direct actionists," and the Right-dominated State Committee, led by John G. Willert of Cleveland, state secretary, instituted recall proceedings against all SEC members. The recall was rushed through in the middle of the election campaign, and while Ohio citizens were giving Ruthenberg an unprecedented vote for governor, the party membership, confused by the sudden propaganda of slander, recalled him and his co-workers from party office. Having spent his entire time for several months in the governorship campaign, thus building up Socialist influence and prestige to an unprecedented height, he was chagrined by this unexpected development. He maintained a stoic exterior, and his sub-committee on the proposed paper promptly turned over all plans and estimates to the State Committee in a signed report and published the report in the November Ohio *Socialist Bulletin.* The State Committee cancelled the order placed with a printing plant for getting out the first issue of the Ohio *Socialist,* and postponed the inaugurating of the paper "to a future date to be hereafter determined." Thus the Right wing of Ohio halted the campaign for a party press. The Ohio *Socialist* finally saw the light of day four years later, in 1916, under sponsorship of Ruthenberg and a new co-worker from the far west, Alfred Wagenknecht, who was elected State Secretary. It wasn't until then that the see-saw struggle between Left and Right in Ohio was finally resolved in favor of the Left.

The recall of Ruthenberg and his colleagues on the Ohio SEC was part of a concerted national drive by the Right to get leading militants out of party leadership. The center of the Ohio Left was in Local Cleveland. Had Ruthenberg set himself to fight the recall proceedings in time—which would have meant an interruption of his governorship campaign—the recall referendum could easily have been defeated. As it was, the state-wide referendum vote was close: 1,095 in favor of recalling the SEC and 971 against, as reported in October.[4] But Local Cleveland counted 2,470 dues-paying members in good standing in that same month! A mobilization of the membership in Cleveland alone would have smashed the recall maneuver.

The pretext for the attack on the SEC was the latter's action in removing certain names from the state speakers' list. The Right-wingers claimed that all speakers who favored "political action" had been taken off the "approved list," and only those who favored "direct action" were allowed to speak in the party's name. The original source of this charge was a scandal story in one of the capitalist papers of Columbus, republished by the Columbus *Socialist,* and then by the Miami Valley *Socialist,* organ of Local Dayton.

Ruthenberg reluctantly took time out from his campaign to answer the charges in a press release, which he thought would take care of the matter. He prefaced his statement with a comment on the character of the attacks against him and his colleagues: "The language of these attacks was so malignant and virulent that one can hardly understand how it could be addressed by one comrade in the Socialist cause to another."

The SEC, Ruthenberg said, had been far from dropping all "political actionists," as the Right-wingers liked to call themselves, though certain speakers it regarded as incompetent were released. Such nationally known "political actionists" as May Wood Simons, Joshua Wanhope and W. F. Barnard were retained on the speakers' list, he said, and so also were editors of the Columbus *Socialist* and the Miami Valley *Socialist,* the papers that had spread the charges in the first place.

Since it was implied that members of the SEC were themselves "direct actionists," Ruthenberg stated: "Personally, I have been speaking in the state every night for more than a month. I challenge those attacking the State Executive Committee to prove that I have in any of these meetings advocated violence as a weapon against the capitalist system."

The Ohio state recall went through, nonetheless, before Election Day, 1912. A Right "Acting State Executive Committee" was appointed by the State Committee for the ensuing months. Ruthenberg did not even dream of leaving the party. He stayed in, worked harder than ever, and bided his time.

A national recall movement against Haywood, superficially similar to but essentially different from the Ohio action, came shortly after the latter. The removal of Haywood from the National Executive Committee, by a referendum instituted in early December, was announced on February 26, 1913. The operation began after Haywood gave a victory speech in Harlem Casino, New York, on December 1, celebrating the "Not Guilty" verdict won by the IWW in the cases of Ettor, Giovanitti, and Caruso, leaders in the Lawrence textile strike who had been accused of murder. The New York *Call* reported, two days after the meeting, that Haywood boasted he *had never advocated political action,* and had openly asserted, "I believe in sabotage, that much misunderstood word." The *Call* and other Socialist papers followed up with attacks on Haywood; New York and New Jersey Right-wingers initiated the recall movement; Haywood's defense was never given to party members—and the recall went through.

In an exhaustive study of this whole incident, Ira Kipnis, author of *The American Socialist Movement, 1897-1912,*[5] concludes that the general charge against Haywood of advocating violence was "highly doubtful." Says Kipnis: "At Lawrence, for example, violence was almost eliminated after Haywood and Ettor took charge of the strike." And as for political action, Haywood had run for governor of Colorado and had campaigned in elections there and in California and elsewhere. Kipnis declares it is "difficult to believe" that Haywood actually said that he " had never advocated" political action. The unmistakable impression one gets from Kipnis' analysis is that the Haywood recall was a far-from-honest political stunt.

But the party members got only the New York *Call* reports on Haywood's speech, reprinted in paper after paper, in most of the states. Ruthenberg himself, who had fought against the "Sabotage Clause" in the party constitution, voted with the majority for Haywood's recall. It was for him a political decision, made on the basis of the available evidence.[6] We must add that the admitted anarcho-syndicalist side of Haywood's theory was beginning to pall on Ruthenberg. The latter's Marxism was becoming sharper and clearer in its application. Incidentally, Debs had left the IWW several years before, and, a little later, Daniel De Leon, Socialist Labor Party leader, also deserted the organization. The un-Marxist aspect of the IWW was leading to its increasing isolation.

In spare moments Ruthenberg continued his reading and study, not only of socialist writings but of current general literature, and in talks to branches or the Young People's Socialist League, he reviewed current novels, and books on science, ethics, economics and politics. Among them in this period were Shaw's *Pygmalion* and Wells' *The Research Magnificent*. Such reading helped to rest and refresh his spirit, and stimulated his mind in efforts to solve the baffling organizational problems that faced him. For he was not without moments of near-discouragement in those difficult days. There were times when he felt heartsick over the hindrances that self-seekers put in the path of the workers. Yet on October 28, 1912, he was able to write to Ann Minturn, a young Left poet who worked in the party's state office: "Do you really think, once having been an active worker in the revolutionary movement, that it is possible to turn back to the dreary and conventional existence of a self-satisfied money-grubber?"

American imperialism was now on the make, priming itself for war. The government was controlled by the most reactionary financial and industrial oligarchs, who made use of troops even then poised for foreign conquest to massacre workers striking at Ludlow for "more bread and better homes." And at the same time they tricked other workers with paternalistic "profit sharing" and company unions, trying to stall off the progressive-minded with fake reforms. "Already," Ruthenberg wrote in the New York *Call*, February 2, 1913, "we have an effort by the capitalists to seize this progressive spirit and to use it to establish a benevolent feudalism, in which the parasitic capitalist class will continue to receive its interest and dividends."

Henry Ford was to go in for "benevolent feudalism" on a big scale at Detroit, with his advertised "five dollars a day" pay, only eleven months after Ruthenberg wrote these words. This was the Ford who, in future days, was to promote anti-Semitism in his own newspaper, The Dearborn *Independent;* who, through his private police force, was to club his workers when they tried to organize; who, two decades later, was to help subsidize Hitler fascism. Quite a few Socialists at this time, Right-wingers chiefly, fell for the Ford myth. Allan L. Benson, who was to be Socialist candidate for President in 1916, became one of Ford's admirers.[7] There was much chatter in the press of "Ford vs. Marx," and assertions that socialism was outdated. Such talk never fazed Ruthenberg.

In June, 1913, Ruthenberg became the combined "organizer and secretary" of Local Cleveland, on a volunteer basis. The position of organizer had been a full-time functionary's job, the only paid post in the local. Ruthenberg refused the salary. He *had* a job—estimate man for the Webster Construction Company. Yet he managed to be the most efficient organizer the Local ever had, in addition to acting as secretary—as he had been doing for three years—and editing the local party publications. And now, while the Left-Right struggle for control of the state went on, Ruthenberg concentrated on the multiple work of recruiting and training class-conscious party workers in Cleveland. He also studied a problem which the National Committee had evaded—that of giving real help in the trade union struggles, which reached the boiling point just before the First World War.

By this time Ruthenberg had developed a theory of party building, which he formulated in the Cleveland *Socialist Party Yearbook* of 1914. "The greatest strength of any organization," he said, "lies in the number of people it attracts who are willing to make sacrifices to increase its strength." Pointing out that in the Socialist movement these people were the active, dues-paying members of the party, he continued: "It is the party members who distribute the literature, solicit subscriptions, organize meetings, nominate political candidates and circulate petitions to place them on the ticket. It is the party members who pay for the leaflets distributed and maintain the party headquarters. The party members are the advance guard, the fighting squadron of the Socialist movement."

His election as "organizer and secretary" was on Monday evening, July 7. Twenty-four hours later he brought out the first issue of his *Party Bulletin,* a weekly typewritten letter, manifolded, to active members. The third issue announced that 80,000 copies of the party's local election platform would be printed—enough to put a copy in "every home in Cleveland." When the platform leaflets were ready, the *Party Bulletin* said: "Cooperation of the entire Party membership will make it possible to distribute these platforms in an hour's time."

More and more the party in Cleveland responded to Ruthenberg's enthusiasm. When enough signatures were secured to put a mayoralty candidate on the ballot, he wrote in the July 28 *Party Bulletin*: "This shows that the party organization is in a healthy condition, and presages aggressive work during the municipal campaign." A month later, because of a change in regulations due to a "non-partisan" provision in the city's new charter, the job had to be done all over again. New petitions had to be circulated, and 2,500 signatures—ten times as many as before—had to be gotten to put the party's candidates on the "non-partisan" ballot. Ruthenberg announced the new requirements in the August 26 *Party Bulletin* and said the work would have to be done fast. And it *was* done fast. By September 23, 4,000 signatures had been collected.

Ruthenberg believed in distribution of literature on a mass scale, with every party member involved. On October 22, the week after 20,000 copies of the party's municipal platform were distributed, he called on the membership to pass out 60,000 copies of another campaign leaflet, entitled "You Have Only One Choice." During the summer he urged the branches to hold open-air meetings. He himself spoke constantly at street gatherings. "The way to make the membership grow is to agitate," he insisted.

Regard for Cultural Activities

It was not only his driving force and his ability to marshall people for routine tasks that made Ruthenberg a great organizer. "His comradely attitude," says Alfred Wagenknecht, who worked with him from about 1915 on, "made him an efficient organizer, exactly because he drew comrades closer in cooperation for the tasks ahead and instilled in them pleasure and enjoyment in the work."

Ruthenberg knew from his own feelings that people in the movement need a social and cultural life. He undertook to provide it by setting up regular Sunday night forums at party headquarters. He explained in the 1914 *Socialist Year Book*: "Within the shell of the present social system we can bring into existence a working class organization with new social ideals, its own educational institutions, its own means of entertainment and social intercourse, with its own press and pulpit, all serving to bring about . . . a recognized social system under which men and women will joyfully perform the work which will . . . make possible education, recreation and culture for all."

Admission to the Sunday night lectures and musicals was free, but a collection was taken. The hall, which held three or four hundred people, was always crowded. At the first forum, November 2, 1913, Ruthenberg gave his "Reply to Mayor Newton D. Baker," who had just refused an invitation to debate, as he had refused two years before when Ruthenberg first ran for mayor. On another occasion, he reviewed Alfred Russell Wallace's latest book, *Social Environment and Moral Progress*. Stereopticon slides prepared by the *National Rip-Saw*, socialist weekly, showing the development of the capitalist system and of machine production, were purchased by Local Cleveland, and he gave the lecture when they were first shown, Sunday night, May 17, 1914. The Women's Committee gave a play, "How the Vote was Won"; Alfred Wagenknecht talked on "How to Build a Socialist Organization"; Ted Robinson of the *Plain Dealer* staff discussed "Heroism and Militarism"; MacBain Walker gave his oft-repeated lecture, "Organic Evolution."

Prominent lecturers were brought from all over the country for these Sunday nights, including Mayor Lewis J. Duncan of Butte, Montana; Janet Fenimore Korngold, national lecturer on women's problems; Mayor Scott Wilkins of St. Mary's, whom Ruthenberg described as "one of the Ohio Socialist mayors who made good"; Arthur Morrow Lewis, author and lecturer, of Chicago; and George R. Kirkpatrick, author of *War–What For?* Ella Reeve Bloor, Socialist organizer–in later years affectionately referred to by thousands as "Mother Bloor"–came often with first-hand stories of the striking Ohio and Pennsylvania miners.

Ruthenberg built his concept of a working class cultural life, not only around the party headquarters, but also around his own hearth fire. "His home was a gathering place for members," says Harry Checel, one of Cleveland's old-timers. "He had them in for supper, for the evening, for Sunday afternoon. He took them for walks in the woods. Sometimes he held committee or branch meetings at his house. Social gatherings would often develop into discussion meetings, or perhaps wind up with impromptu raffles and fund-raising auctions."

Wagenknecht, too, emphasizes Ruthenberg's "amiable and social character," and his "hankering for poetry and good literature." Ruthenberg "would relax of a Sunday," he recalls, "by going with groups of comrades into the fields and woods near the city, taking advantage of such occasions to quote poetry, share his joy in the grandeur of nature and point out what delight people could get out of life if they were not bound down by capitalism. He knew his wild flowers, which he was fond of gathering in immense bouquets. These he carried back home, or to the party headquarters. Often, after these afternoon rambles, the speaker's table at the Sunday night forums would be bright with Ruthenberg's flowers." Ruthenberg threw his whole being into Socialist work. "After his day's work earning a living," says Wagenknecht, "he appeared every evening, without fail, at the Socialist Party headquarters, where he would work far into the night at party tasks." Even during his lunch hour–Harry Checel adds–he managed often to run into the office for a brief conference or a few moments' work. He felt happy and free, not while he was doing the job that earned his living, but while he was working for the movement.

"There is no more important work to be done than to interest women in the party," he wrote in the *Party Bulletin*. "Woman suffrage is coming. . . . If the result of woman suffrage is not to be retrogression for the party . . . we must now do the work which will make the achievement of political equality by the now disfranchised sex an addition to our strength." When Janet Korngold spoke at a Sunday night forum, Ruthenberg urged women "to help make her meeting a stepping stone toward bringing more women members into the party." He called on the men to "bring wife, sweetheart or some woman friend." Other women speakers included Marguerite Prevey of Akron, nationally known, and Anna K. Storck, Socialist member of the Lorain school board. Boldly breaking with sectarianism, Local Cleveland in April, 1914, formally endorsed the Woman's Suffrage Party's petition for the vote.

Just as consistent was Ruthenberg's interest in children and youth. "Socialist Sunday Schools and Young People's Socialist Leagues," he wrote in the *Party Bulletin* for February 3, 1914, "help to keep children and young people in a Socialist atmosphere." A Young People's Socialist League had been formed in 1907, but had fallen apart. Ruthenberg reorganized it, December 17, 1913, and by February there were fifty members. He supported the young people's affairs, and spoke at their meetings. They held bowling matches, dances, baseball games. During the summer of 1914, they had Sunday morning cross-country hikes, with none other than Ruthenberg as their leader.[8] The Socialist Sunday School of Cleveland held its third annual entertainment on November 9, 1913, with a children's program of songs and recitations. Sunday School sessions and the conferences of the Sunday School Board were included in the weekly roster of party activities. In the 1914 May Day celebration, the Sunday School children rode in wagons, and put on a maypole dance afterward in Acme Hall. Among the children in the Socialist Sunday School was Ruthenberg's own son Daniel, then eight years old.

The Ruthenberg home, Daniel recalls, was always full of

Socialists. Visiting lecturers spent the night there. Available were the latest books on socialism and the latest pamphlets and periodicals. "As I grew older," Daniel says, "I read them all. I also attended all the lectures, study groups and mass meetings of the Socialist Party." Ruthenberg did not make the mistake of too much urging, Daniel remembers. "My father," he told this biographer, "never expressed a desire that I take any part in anything, but allowed me to follow my own inclinations."

Ruthenberg encouraged foreign-born Socialists in Ohio to become citizens, and utilized the *Party Bulletin* of January 20, 1914, to give information on how to obtain naturalization papers. During the 1913 municipal campaign, he proudly announced that "all of the foreign language branches assisted in the circulation of the petitions for mayor."

When Ruthenberg became organizer, he found Local Cleveland in a muddle of debt. On ticket sales alone, the office was more than $800 short; there was no record of who had taken tickets to sell, and members had been careless about turning in the money. The Cleveland *Socialist* was in debt about the same amount, with its financial affairs in a snarl. Dues payments were slack. And on top of everything H. A. Morgan, Ruthenberg's predecessor as organizer, admitted a shortage of $194 in the funds he was supposed to turn over to the Local.

Ruthenberg looked upon sound party financing as a political necessity. He wrote in the *Party Bulletin* of November 11, 1913, "As long as the party has hanging over it a lot of unpaid obligations, its work is bound to be hampered and curtailed." His first measure was to cut down expenses. The Cleveland *Socialist* suspended publication. Local Cleveland was without a newspaper until December 5, 1914, except for two months the following summer, when an arrangement was made for a Cleveland edition of the Hamilton *Workers' Cause*. For the first year of Ruthenberg's activity as organizer, the little *Party Bulletin* was Local Cleveland's only organ. From its first issue, it carried financial statements. Measures of economy were followed up with a long range plan to raise funds, which included scores of money-raising devices, from the sale of 5-

cent coupons to an Annual Ball. Straightening out the finances of Local Cleveland was a long hard pull, but the organization was on a sound financial footing by the summer of 1916. On August 12, the Cleveland *Citizen* published Ruthenberg's victorious announcement that "as compared with our financial condition some time ago, we are rich. . . . Today we do not owe a cent and have a surplus of about $5,400 in the treasury." The first *Socialist Party Year Book* (1914) was designed to raise money through advertising. It appeared several months before the outbreak of World War I, and contained, in addition to Ruthenberg's own summation of Socialist progress in Cleveland, a special contribution, "Democracy and Militarism," by J. Keir Hardie, British Socialist who had just toured America to speak against war. On a back page, the *Year Book* quoted Oscar Wilde's observation on "Charity," from *The Soul of Man Under Socialism.*

The first arrest of Ruthenberg—the man who was to be known in a few years as the most arrested labor leader in America—took place during 1913. The *Citizen* tells the story. "Last Saturday night," runs the account, "C. E. Ruthenberg was arrested by Patrolman Page for speaking at E. 9th Street and Vincent Avenue. Page was acting under instructions from headquarters. After some parleying at the police station between Sergeant Vlach, Attorney Louis Katz and Ruthenberg, the latter was released without any charge being placed against him. Meanwhile the meeting at E. 9th Street continued and Ruthenberg returned and finished his speech before a large audience."[9]

Labor and Imperialism

Cleveland school teachers began an organizational drive in January, 1914, in which Ruthenberg was greatly interested. By March, they had formed a "teachers' club" which was asking more pay, with the support of a "congress of mothers" from the school districts. In May, the teachers' club affiliated as a local with the Cleveland Federation of Labor, becoming the second teachers' union in the United States. (The first was in Chicago.) Ruthenberg addressed their meetings from time to time.

The school board's reply was typical: it dismissed the union leaders. Ruthenberg mobilized the party to arouse public opinion against the school board's action. When school opened in the fall, the ousted teachers were still jobless. In the *People's College News,* October, 1914, Ruthenberg urged the teachers to demand that their colleagues be taken back. "A refusal to surrender on their [the teachers'] part," he wrote, "a demand that they be given protection in their profession and some measure of control over the conditions of employment, will be an inspiration to the workers of Cleveland." The teachers carried their case to the courts, but lost. The union fell apart for the time being. But the struggle of the Cleveland teachers has its place in union history.

Ruthenberg initiated the state-wide fight on behalf of the Ohio coal miners, locked out in 1914 by lawless mine owners. He had visited the mining district in the eastern part of Ohio in his 1912 governorship campaign, and, before that, Ella Reeve Bloor, Socialist Party state organizer and a friend of his, had gone down into the mines to talk to the workers on her 1911 tour.[10] Ruthenberg knew how the miners lived. He gave the facts in the Ohio *Socialist Bulletin* for March-April, 1914. The Ohio miners, he pointed out, were fighting against the "screen system" of the employers, whereby a miner was paid, not for all the coal he mined, but only for that part which would not fall through a screen of a certain mesh. (This was before the miners won the right to their own check-weighman.) The workers demanded pay for all the coal they dug, on the "mine run basis." The screen system, Ruthenberg explained, "gives the operators the opportunity to resort to trickery in order to defraud the miners. The meshes of the screen were usually enlarged. Screens . . . used for a long time develop holes through which the miners' wages disappear."

The miners—in spite of the operators' lobby—had finally succeeded the year before in forcing the state legislature to pass an "anti-screen bill." The operators now closed down the mines rather than obey the law, and announced openly that they would keep them closed until they could get the courts to declare the law "unconstitutional." "Suffering and hunger . . . will soon be widespread in the mining regions," Ruthenberg wrote. In the name of Local Cleveland, he called on the State Executive Committee "to immediately begin a statewide campaign to have the State take over the mines and operate them through the miners' organization," and urged quick action to get the facts before the people.

The callous disregard of labor-protection laws on the part of big employers, and the invariable practice of using the police against the workers in every labor dispute, aroused Ruthenberg's fighting spirit. It was on his motion that the municipal platform adopted by the Ohio Socialist Convention in April, 1913, defiantly declared that "Socialists elected to office shall use their power solely in the interests of the working class." Socialist officials, the platform particularly specified, should use the police power to protect striking workers.

Cleveland Socialists gave vigorous support to outstanding strike struggles throughout the United States, notably in Michigan where gun thugs of the Calumet and Hecla mine owners attacked the IWW-led copper miners. They also gave dynamic leadership in Cleveland itself to the fight for help to jobless workers. There was a beginning economic crisis in 1913-14, on the eve of the first World War, and the Socialists, led by Ruthenberg, demanded free school lunches, free medical services for the unemployed, and unemployment relief.

William Jennings Bryan, Wilson's Secretary of State, created a sensation in May, 1913, by taking official notice of charges made in the German Reichstag by Socialist Karl Liebknecht against Krupp armaments. Liebknecht warned that the Krupp company was propagandizing for war in order to pile up more sales and profits. Bryan virtually made a state matter of a Socialist's accusation that a commercial concern could direct a government's policy against the interests of the people. It made quite a stir in Cleveland, where Liebknecht had spoken from the same platform with Ruthenberg only two years before.

This was a portent of approaching world conflict. The increase in armaments and war appropriations in all the large nations, including the United States, caused apprehension in the labor movement of every country, especially among the Socialists. By April, 1914, a threat of imperialist war in the Western hemisphere developed. At President Wilson's order, United States battleships seized the Mexican port of Vera Cruz. There was again danger of United States intervention in Mexican affairs to protect the investments of American Big Business, endangered by the anti-feudal and anti-imperialist Mexican Revolution.[11]

At almost the same moment that American naval guns were pointed at Vera Cruz, the guns of Colorado militiamen—on behalf of the Rockefeller-owned Colorado Fuel and Iron Company—were firing at the families of striking miners in Ludlow. A telegram from the United Mine Workers at Denver to the Cleveland *Citizen,* April 20, 1914, told of the attack: "Ludlow tent colony, which housed 1,200 Colorado striking coal miners, burned to the ground after four men, three women and seven children were murdered. One hundred and fifty gunmen, in militiamen's uniform and with State equipment, have with six machine-guns kept up a constant attack on men, women and children since daybreak Monday morning. . . . Will you, for God's sake and in the name of humanity, call upon all your citizenship to demand of the President of the United States and both houses of Congress that they leave Mexico alone and come into Colorado to relieve these miners, their wives and children, who are being slaughtered . . . by murderous mine-guards?"

The May Day celebration that year was turned into a demonstration against war. When the May Day demonstrators, after an impressive march of thousands through the city's Public Square, gathered at Acme Hall in the evening, they shouted approval of the declaration Ruthenberg read denouncing the threatening conflict. Reviewing the situation in Mexico and in Colorado, his statement said:

"We extend fraternal greetings to the downtrodden people of Mexico and declare our sympathy with them in their struggle to overthrow their oppressors, whether they be Mexican land owners or American capitalists. We express our horror at the brutalities of the paid assassins of the capitalists in

Colorado and declare that there is more dishonor and disgrace to the American flag in that state than in the pretended insults of the Mexican dictator."

War threats continued, but it was in Europe, rather than in Mexico, that war came. On August 2, with the simultaneous invasion of France by Kaiser-led Germany and of Germany by tsarist Russia, the first World War got under way. Inside of a week, Great Britain was in it, too. The war caused a profound change in the problems and activities of Socialists the world over.

6

FOR PEACE—AND FREE SPEECH

THE WEEK WORLD WAR I began in Europe, the Socialists put on an anti-war demonstration in Cleveland. In a pouring Sunday afternoon rain, August 9, 1914, three thousand people gathered around the bandstand in Wade Park, holding their umbrellas aloft, and roared approval as Ruthenberg denounced this new war for profits.

Ruthenberg guided himself by the resolutions of the last three International Socialist Congresses, at Stuttgart (1907), Copenhagen (1910), and Basle (1912), which characterized modern wars as struggles for markets and for re-division of colonial possessions. Such wars, it was declared, bring great sacrifices and suffering to the peoples of the warring countries. The resolutions therefore pledged the working classes of the world to do everything possible to stop a threatening war, and if war broke out in spite of them, to continue opposing it and bring it to an end. Ruthenberg assumed that the top Socialists of France, Germany and England, in accordance with the Congress resolutions, would lead an active anti-war struggle. Actually, as American workers were soon to learn, most Socialist leaders in Europe became pro-war, and most Socialist representatives in the respective European parliaments voted in favor of war credits. Gradually, as months went by, the truth sank in that the Social Democratic leaders in Europe had betrayed the people and that the Socialist International had collapsed.

The extent of Social Democratic backsliding can be realized by recalling the resolution that these very leaders had voted for at an international emergency conference in Basle, in 1912, two years before World War I began. "If a war threatens to break out," the Basle resolution said, "it is the duty of the working classes and their parliamentary representatives in the countries involved, supported by the co-ordinating activity of the International Socialist Bureau, *to exert every effort in order to prevent the outbreak of war by the means they consider most effective,* which naturally vary according to the sharpening of the class struggle and the sharpening of the general political situation."[1]

The war of 1914-18 was a sure-enough capitalist war—a war of capitalism's final stage, imperialism. Honest and courageous Socialists like Debs and Ruthenberg understood very well the war's capitalist nature. "When I say I am opposed to war," wrote Debs in the *Appeal to Reason,* September 11, 1915, in explaining his stand against American entry into World War I, "I mean ruling-class war, for the ruling class is the only class that makes war."[2]

Lenin carried the analysis of just and unjust wars further, and showed that wars of national and colonial liberation should be considered worthy of support. Lenin reserved his severest censure for the wars of modern imperialism that began with the United States war against Spain in 1898-99 and the British war against the South African Boers in 1899-1902.

Ruthenberg stood firm on the Basle resolution from the very first. He scanned the papers to see what the European Socialists were doing. He read with pride of Karl Liebknecht's uncompromising stand in the German Reichstag against junkers and Right Social Democrats alike. Liebknecht, in contrast to many other Socialists in both Germany and France, voted against the war budget. Ruthenberg had no opportunity to read Lenin's current writings on the nature of war and imperialism, but he saw that this was a capitalist war, against the interests of the workers. He became a most insistent voice against the war, a most steadfast spokesman for the Left.

In the early months of the European conflict, as it happens, the immediate threat of United States involvement in war was south of the Rio Grande rather than across the Atlantic. President Woodrow Wilson's arrogant policy toward our southern neighbor drew sharp criticism from the Socialist Party. Socialist spokesmen were at this time more aware of the threatened American aggression against Mexico than of possible involvement in a world conflict. But the European war brought visions of large orders from belligerent countries to American manufacturers, bankers and dealers in military supplies. It multiplied the cost of living. It gave Big Business an excuse to foist militarism on the country and attempt to suppress organized labor. It was by leading a fight on these issues that Ruthenberg built the mass support in Cleveland which made possible that city's outstanding struggle against imperialist reaction when in 1917 the war engulfed America.

Three months after the European war began, while Ruthenberg was trying to find his way in the midst of new problems, his mother died. She passed away November 21, 1914, at the age of 68.

"Starve the War and Feed America"

When the war started in Europe, prices rose in America. Before August, 1914, was over, the Socialist National Committee demanded that the government seize food supplies held by speculators and halt the export of munitions and money. The slogan was, "Starve the War and Feed America!" Cleveland's Socialists approved the slogan. They held a mass meeting in Public Square on September 6 and distributed 50,000 copies of the "Starve the War" leaflet.

Five-cent bread became a thing of the past. Meat consumption in Cleveland declined 40 per cent. Between September, 1915, and September, 1916, food prices—it was said, locally—jumped 30 cents on the dollar. The rising cost of living sharpened the misery of the unemployed. By December, 1914, 61,000 Clevelanders were looking for work. That was one city's share of a growing army of unemployed. One of capitalism's periodic breakdowns was at hand, and the war, by disrupting industry, had—at least for the time being—aggravated the "hard times."

Unemployment in the city had tripled in the year just past. Stores in working class neighborhoods reported that workers' charge accounts had increased 700 per cent. Associated Charities was swamped with appeals for aid. On one Monday morning —December 21—a police check-up at fifty factory gates showed that 2,891 men applied for work, and only sixty were hired. At Christmas time, a teenage boy was shot and killed by a grocer for stealing a bun. As early as December 13, the Socialist Party of Cleveland drew up a plan to meet the critical unemployment situation. A letter to the City Council demanded free eating places for the unemployed, relief stations to supply clothing and fuel, provision for emergency housing, and increased appropriations for public works to provide jobs. Copies of this letter, signed by Ruthenberg, were published by the Cleveland *Citizen* and the Cleveland *Federationist,* liberal and conservative weeklies, respectively, of the local AFL. The Cleveland Federation of Labor endorsed the Socialist demands.

Ruthenberg strode into a hearing of the City Council in January, 1915, and demanded that the city appropriate a half million dollars to feed and house the homeless. "The little men who are managing the city's affairs are afraid of the unemployed problem," he told the Councilmen. A special "Unemployed Edition" of the *Socialist News,* Ruthenberg's new party paper, was gotten out on January 16. The party received support on this issue from the city's trade unions, whose jobless membership had doubled. Ruthenberg was invited by the Amalgamated Iron and Steel Workers local, January 17, to discuss the question, "How Can We Save the Working Class from Unemployment?" Mayor Newton D. Baker was forced to set up a committee on unemployment. Every man he appointed was a big employer. This crew of big business men met daily over lunch and Havana cigars at the Hollenden Hotel. They ended by announcing that many who called themselves unemployed were "insincere," that the problem was "too complicated" to solve anyhow, and that workers who had jobs should each donate a day's pay. They also started a "hire-a-man" movement, through which they got jobs for 750 out of the 61,000 jobless by mid-February, when they disbanded.

Not one of the big employers hired a single extra man. The Baker administration did not appropriate a penny for relief.

The Chamber of Commerce announced in its annual report that business was normal for 1914. "Interesting, isn't it?" Ruthenberg commented in the *Socialist News*. " 'It is not to die, or even to die of hunger, that makes a man wretched,' " he quoted Thomas Carlyle; " 'it is to live the life miserable, we know not why; to work sore, and yet gain nothing; to be heartworn, weary, yet isolated, girt in with a cold universal *laissez faire*.' "

It was in the *Socialist News* of March 6, 1915, that Ruthenberg thus quoted Carlyle. Fifteen years later, March 6, 1930, at the depth of a greater crisis, Communist-led demonstrations throughout the country forced the granting of federal unemployment relief. The leaders of these demonstrations told the unemployed: "You have a *right* to live. You have a right to *fight* to live."

Cooperative food buying was first discussed in Local Cleveland in the spring of 1915. A year later, Ruthenberg called an organizational meeting in his office, and on May 29, 1916, the Cooperators' Company was launched, with Ruthenberg as treasurer. While there were three other cooperatives in Cleveland which served the purposes of economy just as well, the Cooperators' Company had a political function also. One of its first acts was to vote $10 for the defense of Socialists arrested for anti-war activity.

Socialist-Labor Cooperation

The growing friendliness of the Cleveland Federation of Labor toward the Socialist May Day celebrations is a rough measure of the cooperation Ruthenberg was now able to develop between party and unions. Every spring, a formal invitation to march on May Day went from Local Cleveland to the CFL central body. In earlier years the invitation had been regularly tabled. In 1914 the chairman of the central body, according to the Cleveland *Federationist*, stated that "any locals desiring to participate in this event could do so"; in 1915, those who wished to were "requested to attend"; in 1916, "those who could *should* take part." More and more union locals marched under their own banners in the parade.

In the summer and fall of 1915, Cleveland Socialists made new and more determined efforts to work in the unions. The Sixth Ward Branch, July 24, devoted a meeting to "Should a Socialist Talk Socialism in the Shop?" On August 21, the 24th Ward Branch considered, "How Can the Socialist Party Bring About Better Relations With the Unions?" In October, while the machinists' strike was on, John Luthringer, national organizer of the Machinists' Union, addressed the party's City Central Committee. The *Socialist News* on April 29, 1916, announced the setting up of a preliminary Labor Union Committee, including representatives of the Machinists, Auto workers, and Slaters and Tile Roofers. The Committee called for suggestions from the rank and file, to be mailed to Ruthenberg's office. On May 18, Socialist trade unionists met at headquarters to plan further work within the unions. The following week the Labor Union Committee circularized CFL locals offering educational lectures free of charge, an offer which was accepted by several unions. The cooperation thus stimulated was interrupted by the anti-labor terror which accompanied America's entry into the war less than two years later.

The sinking of the *Lusitania,* May 7, 1915, by a German submarine was a signal to American munitions-makers and militarists to start a pro-war campaign. It brought home the realization that the United States, whose capitalists were getting rich by selling war-goods to both sides, might get into the war. When the Lusitania went down, 1,195 people died. But, as Ruthenberg pointed out in the *Socialist News,* 8,672 were killed or crippled every year in the State of Ohio alone, through industrial accidents, and nobody said a word. War contracts made the industrial accident rate leap. In June, 1916, there were 800 more accidents in Ohio factories than in any month since records had been kept.

The Socialist Party won the friendship of many trade unionists that summer by its support of the local AFL's campaign for a minimum wage for city employees. City officials were getting big pay raises to meet rising living costs, but city laborers still received only $2.00 a day. The CFL wanted a minimum of $2.50. A minimum wage amendment to the city charter, however, was needed, and this meant collecting signatures to petitions to force a referendum vote. In April, after the CFL endorsed the move by Carpenters' Local 11 for such an amendment, Ruthenberg got out the whole Socialist Party to collect signatures. On August 21, the CFL announced that over 3,000 signatures—far more than half the number needed—had been turned in by "Secretary C. E. Ruthenberg of the Socialist Party." The amendment was submitted to a referendum, and passed.

This cooperation was not thrown away. The Federation's vice-president, Thomas J. Dolan, told the Cleveland *Citizen* that Ruthenberg would get his vote for Mayor. Without the help of Ruthenberg and the Socialists, "we could not have had the required per cent of signers to put it [the amendment] to a vote of the people," Dolan said.

The Luna Park Labor Day celebration showed that other union men felt the same way. According to custom, mayoralty candidates of all parties came to Luna Park to tell the workers why they expected labor's vote. Ruthenberg spoke last. Sitting in a row back of him on the platform were the four other candidates, including Newton D. Baker's man, Peter Witt, Democrat, and Republican Harry L. Davis. In the big pavilion, every inch of standing room was taken. Thundering hand-claps welcomed Ruthenberg as he stood up to speak. The faces of the old party candidates reddened, as the ovation swelled and Ruthenberg held up his hand for silence. They blushed still more as he told how "the little men" who ran the city's affairs had denied to the garbage collectors the right to organize, had underpaid the electrical workers, had dodged the demand for a minimum wage. "You're right!" the crowd shouted, "That's the truth!"

Cleveland workers struck against the speed-up and the rising cost of living. In the midst of the strike wave, the Austrian ambassador had the effrontery to call on American munitions workers of Austrian descent to down tools. The war profiteers welcomed his indiscretion. The strikers are pro-German, they blared.

Ruthenberg made short work of this attack on organized labor. "Of course," he wrote, "any working man who will go on strike to help the ruling class of any of the capitalist nations gain an advantage in the game of murder is worse than a fool, but there is no reason under the sun why the workers should not take advantage of the present situation to gain better wages and working conditions for themselves. . . . They should prepare to strike, not to help Austria or Germany against the Allies, or the reverse, but in order to make the capitalists yield up to them a larger share of what they are producing through their labor power." The workers at the Cleveland Automatic Machine Company were striking at a most favorable moment, he said, when they called a stoppage early in October, 1915. "To have the work of production interrupted means a loss of big profits," he said, "and this threatened loss will move the capitalists to make concessions. quicker than anything under the sun."

Socialist Perspective

Ruthenberg himself had never belonged to a union. The white-collar and professional workers in Cleveland at that time were not organized. But experience brought him face to face with the trade union question. In January, 1915, he went to work for the Printz-Biederman Company, one of the largest employers of garment workers in the country. Starting as head of the correspondence department, he soon became office manager. Printz-Biederman workers had been in the big Cleveland garment strike of 1911, which Ruthenberg had made one of the issues of his mayoralty campaign. But the concern had remained unorganized. Later, the management set up a company union known as the "House of Representatives," through which workers in both shop and office were supposed to have a "voice" in their "government."

Ruthenberg was chosen by the office workers as their "representative." His wife Rose recalls the stories he told about this farcical "government." Ruthenberg stood up in the "Representatives'" sessions and told the workers not to be misled by it. "We workers have the authority to decide how many spittoons we may have, and where to put them," he said. "But the company decides all the really important questions like wages and hours. They decide when and whom to fire. If the questions we decide haven't any importance at all, we can talk forever!"

In these years he was searching for a Socialist solution of trade union problems, as shown by his article, "The Work Before Us," in the *Socialist Year Book,* Cleveland, 1916. "We must bring into harmony with the political and cooperative movement the industrial wing of the workers' organizations," he wrote, disregarding the official Socialist policy of neutrality in trade union matters. "How this is to be achieved the future alone can tell, but we must keep it in our minds as part of the end to be sought." Ruthenberg left the Printz-Biederman Company two and a half years afterward, in June, 1917. Still later, in the winter of 1919—to look ahead for a moment—while its workers were again waging an organizing battle, he started a clerks' union for its office workers and salesmen, and joined it himself. On March 1, 1919, the *Socialist News* announced that the Retail Clerks' Fraternal Association had been formed. The "Ruthenberg local," as it came to be called, was admitted to the Cleveland Federation of Labor as a local of the Bookkeepers, Stenographers and Accountants Union (BSAU-AFL), but later was kicked out—a victim of post-war redbating.

Despite Ruthenberg's Party jobs and his responsibilities at Printz-Biederman's, he continued to run for office every year—in 1914 for congressman, in 1915 for mayor again, in 1916 for U.S. Senator. His fellow Socialists, fired by his example, strove loyally to help the work. Every Thursday night, when the *Socialist News* was printed, party members came to headquarters for the mailing. They sent out announcements of the Sunday night forums and other meetings, appeals for funds, for canvassers. The mailing bees continued week in and week out, year after year, under the direction of the Women's Committee.

Among the devoted workers were Jacob Heinrich and his family. On one occasion Heinrich, after selling forty tickets to a Debs meeting, armed himself with a campaign donation list and went out to visit his relatives. In a few hours he came back with twenty-one donations from twenty-one Heinrichs, and brought his daughters with him to help with the mailing bee.

Ruthenberg enjoyed Socialist work. When his friend, Ann

Minturn, who had dropped out of political activity to write poetry, urged him not to martyr himself, he answered, in a letter dated January 27, 1915: "I am not a martyr. . . . I am merely doing the work out of which I get the greatest joy. I believe in the organized working class movement. While we may blunder and stumble, I am confident that we are moving toward our goal."

Poetry never tempted Ruthenberg to quit work—it aroused him to work the harder. To the same friend, he wrote in April, "What power is there in these poets and dreamers that they can arouse us to attack the bars of the cage we have ourselves built?" The poet who most inspired him in these years was William Morris. Often in his speeches he quoted a stanza or so from *The Day Is Coming* or *The Voice of Toil.*[3]

For a long time now, Ruthenberg had been working on a pamphlet to make clear to American readers the Marxist theory of the necessity of socialism. The pamphlet, entitled *Are We Growing Toward Socialism?* was given to the printer early in 1917, before the United States entered the World War. Daniel Ruthenberg remembers how, at the age of twelve, he read the page proofs. Instead of lecturing his son on socialism, C. E. offered him a quarter for every printer's error he could find—and got him to read the pamphlet.

Are We Growing Toward Socialism? did not speculate on whether the human race could effortlessly drift into the future. Despite certain shortcomings, it was a scientific demonstration that socialism is the next step in social evolution; it was a militant call to action. "Are we the plaything of fate which is bringing into the world a new chaos for us to struggle in?" he asked, pointing to the frightening growth of vast corporations, which foreshadowed a new tyranny. Putting his trust in man's inherent fighting spirit, he answered: "Men have never willingly accepted the yoke of slavery. They have always fought for freedom. In a society in which an enslaved class exists, there will always be a class conflict." "Socialism grows as the water lily grows," he wrote in conclusion. "At the bottom of the lakes and ponds in which the water lily grows there is deposited a muck of decaying vegetable matter. In this the water lily sets its roots. . . . Out of this muck it sends up its stem through the waters which surround it, upward to the light and air and sunshine, and when it reaches the light and air and sunshine, it bursts forth into that beautiful blossom which gives us joy to behold. The Socialist Movement sets its roots in the muck of capitalism. It finds in it the conditions which enable it to live and thrive. Today the Socialist Movement is fighting its way upward, upward against the lies, misrepresentation and the misunderstanding which surround it, upward to the light and air and sunshine. Soon it will reach the light and air and sunshine, and then our civilization will burst forth into that new and beautiful blossom—Socialism."

The Debate on War

Buccaneering finance-capital, striding with seven-league boots, was dragging the United States into the war. United States capitalists were supplying goods at great profit to both warring alliances. The war was thus changing this country from a debtor to a creditor nation, making it the money-master of the world. From coast to coast, "Military preparedness" became the cry of Big Business. The Pacific Coast Business Men's Preparedness League put the case baldly, demanding "adequate troops . . . to deal with domestic strife and to suppress probable labor uprisings."[4] Attacks on organized labor multiplied. In January, 1916, striking iron and steel workers were shot down in Youngstown, Ohio. In July, a provocateur's bomb thrown at a San Francisco military preparedness parade led to a frame-up; and Tom Mooney, a Socialist trade unionist, was sentenced to be hanged. A fellow unionist, Warren K. Billings, was sent to prison for life. The drive was on for U. S. entry into the war.

Eugene V. Debs, in the *National Rip-Saw,* December 1915, expressed his grief and anger at the turncoat Second International. "That the International *did* collapse, and utterly so, when the crucial test came, it were folly any longer to deny or attempt to extenuate," he wrote. "The day may be nearer than we imagine when we, here in the United States, will have to prove ourselves and the fitness of our movement to survive the onslaught of the murderous military hordes of capitalism."

A month later a colleague of Lenin, Alexandra Kollontay, then on a lecture-tour of the United States, published an article in the *International Socialist Review* in which she called on American Socialists to support a proposed new International. In later articles in the same magazine, S. J. Rutgers, a Dutch Socialist then in America, and familiar with Lenin's writings, explained the imperialist nature of the war, and showed why revolutionary Socialists were obliged to break completely with the "social patriots" who had led the Second International to disaster. The new set-up, it was explained, was proposed at the Zimmerwald Conference in Switzerland, September, 1915, where Socialists who refused to compromise with the war tried to reconstruct the International. At that Conference, a minority group led by Russian delegates insisted that a new International, starting from scratch, was essential. It was Lenin who organized that minority at Zimmerwald.

It was through Rutger's articles that Ruthenberg and others in this country first began to get an inkling of Lenin's teachings about imperialism, and a real understanding of the origin and nature of wars under capitalism, though it was not until 1919 that the first English translation of Lenin's *Imperialism, the Final Stage of Capitalism,* written in 1916, was brought out in Boston.[5] The imperialist nature of the European War was established much earlier by Lenin in various current publications, speeches and resolutions, 1914-15, in the very first year of the conflict; but except for a few short articles which appeared in the press, these did not become available in English until the '20's when the publication of Lenin's *Collected Works* began in this country.

Throughout the American Socialist Party a heated debate arose in 1915 over the party's attitude toward the war. Many Right leaders, like their prototypes in Europe, were shifting to a pro-war stand. Debs, who had headed the Socialist ticket in three national election campaigns, declined to be the 1916 nominee for president. Charles Edward Russell, a prominent publicist, who had written voluminously in opposition to the war in Europe, was nominated for president in a Socialist Party referendum. In the meantime, as American participation came closer, he switched over and came out openly for the war, and was at once not only recalled as presidential nominee—in another referendum—but expelled from the party. There was still time to nominate Allan L. Benson, another anti-war publicist, who became the Socialist Standard-bearer for 1916. But Benson, too—almost in the middle of his campaign—began to straddle the war issue.

The Right-Left cleavage on the war was obvious as early as January, 1916, when the N. Y. *Call* asked Socialist candidates for the National Committee to state their position on the "Question of Militarism." Benson, candidate for President, came out with a few words about not increasing the Army or Navy. The Reverend W. R. Gaylord of Wisconsin offered a program of "preparedness for peace." Many of the declarations were high-sounding evasions. Ruthenberg, as a candidate for National Committeeman, wrote: "It is our work to show that [capitalist war] is a fruit of an industrial system based upon production for profit, with all that that implies in the shape of competition with the capitalists of other nations, and to oppose it with all our power. If we compromise at this point it will open the way for greater compromises. I am unalterably opposed to militarism and preparedness in all its forms." Other Left voices were heard The late Robert Minor, great cartoonist and war correspondent for the *Call*, just back from the fighting fronts, warned on a speaking tour—which took in Cleveland—that Wall Street plotted to send American soldiers to Europe to collect the millions loaned to the Allies.[6]

Events moved fast all over the world that spring of 1916. In Ireland, Socialists and other patriots rose against British imperialism in the Easter Rebellion. James Connolly, its leader, an Irish Socialist who less than a decade earlier had lived in New York and lectured in Cleveland, was murdered by the British government after the uprising was crushed.

May Day came to Cleveland. In its parade—as the scandalized *Plain Dealer* recorded—one placard read: "We refuse to fight in any war but that for working class freedom." In a May Day editorial in the *Socialist News*, Ruthenberg wrote: "The 'times that try men's souls' [Thomas Paine] are before the workers of this country: Capitalism, in its logical development, has turned Europe into a nightmare of bloodshed and destruction. . . .

"In America we have thus far escaped this, capitalism's most terrible fruit, but the chasm yawns before us, ready to engulf us in the sea of blood. . . .

"Capitalism . . . is fighting to replace democracy in this country with a military machine. . . . There is no middle ground for us. . . We are not to be deluded by the sham cries of 'preparedness' advocates . . .

"We stand for the patriotism of humanity, which welcomes the people of all nations into the circle of human brotherhood.

"We will not fight except to resist and wipe out of existence the ugliest thing the world has produced—the capitalist system and the capitalist class."

Intervention in Mexico

In March, 1916, with the United States teetering on the edge of the war in Europe, American troops crossed into Mexico. It was this expedition that brought out Brigadier General John J. Pershing as imperialist America's military leader, and prepared him for the world war that the U. S. was to enter a year later. This invasion of Mexican soil was on the pretext of running down Pancho Villa, the Mexican peasant-patriot, whom American Big Business called a "bandit."[7] The Cleveland Socialists announced a meeting in the Central Armory with Debs as speaker, to denounce the invasion.

On June 29 a *Plain Dealer* editorial called for suppression of Socialist speakers in the Public Square. It told Public Safety Director A. B. Sprosty: "Stop all speeches on the Public Square attacking the United States flag, National Guardsmen or the attitude of the Government in the Mexican crisis." Republican Mayor Harry L. Davis, then in the saddle, was behind the new policy. Within twenty-four hours Socialist workers were beaten on the Public Square by men in uniform for saying the invasion of Mexico was a disgrace to the American flag. The police stood around without lifting a finger. Another twenty-four hours, and Ruthenberg answered Public Safety Director Sprosty by holding an emergency mass meeting on the Square. The press was notified that the American assault on Mexico would be discussed.

A thousand people were there. Ruthenberg mounted the stone block, traditional free speech rostrum at the foot of Tom Johnson's statue. Not a policeman was in sight, but armed militiamen began to push their way toward the platform.

As Ruthenberg told of the oil and banking interests that were back of the attack on Mexico, the crowd cheered. "There is no reason," his voice rang out, "why any man should go down into the hell of war to fight for the dollars of the ruling class!" As he said this, the militiamen rushed for the rostrum, using the butt ends of their revolvers to strike down all in their way. The crowd fought back with bare fists.

Some Socialists went to call the police, while Ruthenberg held his place. A half dozen policemen sauntered into the Square some ten minutes later, and the fighting let up. Ruthenberg spoke again, then introduced Tom Clifford, Socialist candidate for governor. "It was only through the determined stand of the Socialist Party," Ruthenberg wrote in the next issue of the *Socialist News*, "That the right of free speech from the public rostrum was reestablished and maintained."

Another Public Square meeting was called for Sunday, July 9, and the Socialist Labor Party and the Cleveland Federation of Labor were invited to take part. The SLP sent speakers, and while the CFL gave no official support hundreds of union members were there. This time the Square bristled with police, on horseback and motorcycle and afoot. The meeting was not interrupted. That same week, a gang of toughs including militia in uniform, led by one City Councilman Taylor, assaulted a Socialist soapboxer at the corner of Kinsman and East 93rd Street, and broke up the meeting. Again the police watched the attack and did nothing. Ruthenberg at once gave notice that he would himself be the speaker at Kinsman and East 93rd on July 11, and invited Councilman Taylor to be there. When the night come, more than five hundred people showed up to listen to the Socialist city organizer. But not Taylor. There was no disorder.

All summer attacks on street meetings continued. The police themselves began to interfere with speakers. Whenever trouble occurred at a street corner, Ruthenberg spoke there the next week. Finally, late in August, at Chestnut and East 9th Street, while five hundred people were listening to William Francis Barnard, one of Local Cleveland's lecturers, the cop on the beat interrupted to tell the speaker it was against the law to sell literature. Ruthenberg walked up at that moment, picked up some copies of the *International Socialist Review,* mounted the speaker's stand and announced to the crowd that he was going to test the ruling. He sold three copies as fast as he could hand them out, then followed the cop to police headquarters.

At the station, the red-faced sergeant said he had orders from higher up to stop the selling of literature on the street. Someone had dug up a city ordinance about peddling without a license. Ruthenberg told him the Socialist Party had been holding street meetings and selling literature for ten years, and intended to keep right on. Another meeting, he said, would be held the next night at the same corner, and literature would be sold. After some blustering, the sergeant let Ruthenberg go. The following night's meeting was not molested. In spite of these efforts to terrorize the Party, it kept on growing. Between May and November, 77 new members joined.

Many still tell of Ruthenberg's courageous leadership that summer, and of the feeling of confidence his poise gave them. "He always looked so wonderful when he stood up, so in command of the situation," said Ella Reeve Bloor, years later. "I don't think he had one minute of fear."

Yetta Land, Cleveland's labor attorney, tells of the quiet smile with which he met danger. "On a sunny October day in 1916," she says, "at a meeting in Market Square, Ruthenberg was speaking from my car. Police officers stood all around us threateningly, in front of the crowd. The sun on their badges kept flashing in Ruthenberg's eyes. After a while he asked, 'Will the police officers please get in back of me? Your badges are bothering my eyes.' And then, with a faint smile, 'But please leave your sticks here.' A few minutes later, he repeated, 'Would the *gentlemen* police officers please move back—and you can take your sticks along with you!' "

Railwayman Bruce Smith, Socialist member of the Toledo City Council who stood his ground when the war came, remembers: "Ruthenberg had a faculty for taking the hide and hair off the militarists. At the same time, he was one of the most kindly men I ever met. He had a mild smile, a smile to remember, and a come-let-us-reason-together voice, a sort of nice bass voice. He was a very heroic person, a wonderful advocate of a better world to live in."

In "The Hour of Decision," Cleveland *Socialist News* editorial, November 4, 1916, Ruthenberg wrote:

"The people of this country face the most momentous election day since the days before the Civil War. . . . Despite all the petty bickerings and puerile arguments on the part of the Republican and Democratic candidates, the two big vital questions before the voters are *militarism and hard times.* Shall this country be turned from its peaceful development of democracy into a military autocracy? . . . Shall we have security or insecurity? Shall we keep the industries running to produce what we need, or shall we have periodical unemployment and hard times?"

7

"NOT A WAR FOR FREEDOM"

IN THE SPRING OF 1917 the United States got into the War. President Wilson, re-elected in 1916 because "He Kept Us Out of War," cut diplomatic relations with Germany on the following February 3rd. The jingo press howled for conscription. Wilson convened a special session of Congress for mid-April to declare war.

The Socialist membership had been clamoring for the party to take a stand on the war, and the National Executive Committee had initiated a referendum looking toward a national convention during the summer. When the special session of Congress was announced, the party's executive, realizing delay would be fatal, called an Emergency Convention at St. Louis for April 7.

In Cleveland, beginning in February, Ruthenberg called a series of big anti-war rallies. At the third of these, held March 1 in Moose Hall, he shared the platform with Eugene V. Debs. Worried by the way people flocked to Ruthenberg's anti-war meetings, the Cleveland Chamber of Commerce held a "loyalty mass meeting" March 12 at Gray's Armory, where very little popular war fever was steamed up.

Then, two days later, March 14, on the other side of the world, the people of Russia kicked out Tsar Nicholas II. Alarmed by this overturn, which weakened the Eastern Front of Allied imperialism in its war against German imperialism, President Wilson set the special session two weeks earlier, on April 2nd. But Ruthenberg—unlike the President—was happy over the Russian Revolution, and strengthened by it. The people's victory against the Tsar steeled him in his anti-war stand.

Discerning people had seen for weeks that the United States

would enter the war, not only to protect loans to the Allies but to take part in the re-division of spoils that was bound to come at the war's end. But the public had to be brought around to a warlike mood; a show had to be staged, to hide the war-makers. As Congress met, Big Business plugged for war. New York *Times* headlines for the first week in April tell the story: "Strike Hard in War," the National City Bank urged on April 2, though war was not yet declared. April 4 headlines: "Wall Street Ready With War Billions—Prepared to Help the Government Without Remuneration." On inside pages: "Rockefeller Praises Wilson. . . . President's Address Endorsed in Wall Street —'Exactly Right,' Judge [Steel Trust] Gary's Comment. . . . [Herbert] Hoover Thanks Wilson."

"You Will Pay in Blood and Suffering," Ruthenberg warned in a leaflet on April 1. That rainy Sunday morning, the Socialists of Cleveland handed to their fellow townsmen 50,000 copies of this warning. The leaflet quoted, ironically, a Republican electioneering statement of only a year before, which had appeared over the signatures of two ex-presidents, Theodore Roosevelt and William Howard Taft: "The rivalries that begin in commerce end on the battlefield. The history of war is green with international jealousies." The leaflet went on, in Ruthenberg's words: "It is the workers who will pay the cost of the war. . . . The capitalists will make more profits. The Socialists of Cleveland call upon all the men and women who are opposed to killing their fellow human beings to protect the 'property rights' of the capitalist class to join them in demanding peace."[1]

That afternoon, a stop-the-war mass meeting was scheduled at Gray's Armory. Cleveland's daily papers declared in headlines that the meeting was called off, but 2,000 Clevelanders believed the leaflet, and showed up at the Armory in a pouring rain. The Armory doors were locked. The management, although paid in advance, had cancelled the meeting. The crowd followed Ruthenberg to the Public Square. It "put new courage" in the hearts of those who were against war, as Ruthenberg reported in the next issue of the *Socialist News*, "to see the lines of umbrellas, covering a multitude of people stretching out and down Ontario Street as far as the eye could reach," and then to see this "same umbrella-covered multitude," stand in the mud and water, soaked through by the rain, and cheer and applaud the speakers for peace.

The Cleveland *Plain Dealer,* the day after the demonstration, reported in a front page story that Ruthenberg told the crowd: "This is not a war of peoples. It is a capitalists' war, and the war-mongers of the Chamber of Commerce, and the editors, sitting back in easy chairs, will find the strongest indictment of it in the Declaration of Independence."

On the evening of April 2, the day Congress convened, Cleveland Socialists celebrated the overthrow of tsarism in Russia. In the East Technical High School auditorium where the celebration was held, a crowd of 2,500 cheered Ruthenberg's declaration for "fraternity and internationalism."

Ruthenberg knew the road ahead would not be easy. He knew about the French Socialist leader, Jean Jaurès, shot by an assassin as he cried, "Down with the War!"; about the German Socialists, Karl Liebknecht and Rosa Luxemburg, behind the bars of the Kaiser's prison; about the murdered Irish Socialist, James Connolly, victim of British imperialism. "We are being tested by fire," Ruthenberg wrote in the *Socialist News.* "Let us set an example of fidelity to our principles, and send our comrades the world over the inspiring message that at least our section of the international working class has kept faith in the hour of trial."

The St. Louis Convention

On April 6, 1917, Congress declared war on Germany. On that day, Ruthenberg drew up a "Manifesto Against War." When he took the train for St. Louis that afternoon, to attend the National Emergency Convention of the Socialist Party, he left a copy of his Manifesto to be read at a mass meeting. It was adopted by Local Cleveland and published in the *Socialist News* while he was away. He had another copy in his pocket for the Convention. On the train to St. Louis with Ruthenberg were six other Ohio delegates, including Alfred Wagenknecht, who had become State Secretary, and Charles Baker, Organizer.

Among the 192 delegates who crowded into the Banquet Hall of the Planters Hotel, St. Louis, on April 7, others besides Ruthenberg carried draft resolutions in their pockets. Morris Hillquit brought one which was in large part the basis for the anti-war declaration finally adopted. Louis Boudin, Socialist theoretician, had another. John Spargo, who did not want a convention held in the first place, brought a resolution endorsing American entry into the war.

For two months before the Convention, Spargo and the Rev. W. R. Gaylord had been writing protest letters to the National Executive Committee every time a Socialist opened his mouth to oppose the war. Spargo resigned from the party shortly after the Convention, and so did the previous year's presidential candidate, Allan Benson. Gaylord was expelled for calling on Government officials to suppress Socialist anti-war propaganda! Within two months, Spargo joined with Charles Edward Russell and others to form the pro-war "American Socialist Party"—which had a very short life indeed. It never functioned as a party. While some inside the Convention were trying to betray the workers to imperialism, renegades outside were taking jobs in the war administration. George Creel, Socialist Party Right wing journalist, accepted President Wilson's appointment as head of the committee for war propaganda.

But the war Socialists were only a handful at the Convention. A bloc of at least sixty Left-wingers from various parts of the country were bent on firm opposition to the war. This group, which included all seven Ohio delegates, followed Ruthenberg's lead at the Convention.

At the outset of the Convention Ruthenberg tried to strengthen this Left bloc by enlisting the support of Gene Debs, whose anti-war stand was well-known. But Debs declined to attend. The story is told by Ray Ginger in *The Bending Cross,* a biography of Debs, as follows: "Their [the Left-wingers'] spokesman, Charles E. Ruthenberg of Ohio, telephoned Debs in Terre Haute and urged him to come to St. Louis. Debs refused. . . . But Ruthenberg was not satisfied. One night he loaded two cars with delegates and drove the hundred and fifty miles to Terre Haute. The trip was made in vain."[2] Debs insisted that his opposition to the war was clear to the delegates, and that his presence was unnecessary.

The Left distrusted the Right for their hesitancy, their evasive and dilatory manner whenever a real fight against reaction had to be faced. Hillquit, typical Centrist, and Berger, typical Right-winger—chiefs of Socialist Party leadership—were unquestionably both opposed to the war at this time, but the Right—or "old guard"—could not be depended on to carry through a militant and determined anti-war struggle. The Left tried to get into its own hands the leadership of the war against war.

In St. Louis, that spring day in 1917, Hillquit made a mournful "keynote" speech, recalling past glories of the Socialist Party. And then, he said, came this "lamentable" war! He spoke of the collapse of the International, but did not name those who were responsible. When, however, he ended by calling for continued opposition to "this criminal war, even now after it has been declared," applause and cries of "Good!" broke from the delegates.

The Convention's chief committee was that on War and Militarism. Its fifteen members included Hillquit, Berger, Spargo, Boudin and Ruthenberg. Its chairman was Kate Richards O'Hare, anti-war agitator of St. Louis. From the start, these spokesmen for differing viewpoints were unable to get together on a single resolution. They split three ways. Spargo went off by himself to mull over his pro-war proposal. Boudin and two others, oblivious of the need for solidarity of the anti-war forces, also withdrew to work out a differently worded against-the-war statement.

Choosing the path that would mean a united working class and mass anti-war action, Ruthenberg was willing to work with Hillquit and Berger if the majority of the delegates could thus be mobilized to support a genuine anti-war resolution.[3] A subcommittee consisting of Hillquit, Ruthenberg and Algernon Lee drew up the majority resolution. Its formulation required four days, and was the subject of violent discussion for two days more. It was adopted the evening of the 12th, receiving

141 votes. The Boudin resolution got 31 votes, and Spargo's pro-war one got five.

The Hillquit-Ruthenberg document, though far from ideal, was a definite anti-war manifesto. It was somewhat heavy with pacifist phraseology. But these weaknesses did not destroy its essence. The fight against the war which it called for could be carried out only through militant mass struggle.

For the most part the resolution was in Hillquit's somewhat florid style. Ruthenberg, however, contributed a considerable part of the fighting content. The Ruthenberg draft was adopted by Local Cleveland as its "Manifesto Against War" before the Hillquit-Ruthenberg resolution was presented at St. Louis. It was published in the *Socialist News* on April 14, before the St. Louis Convention was over.

Ruthenberg's was a shorter, simpler document, although less carefully worked out. While it had some of the faults of the St. Louis declaration, its program of action was more concrete. It did not assume that the fight against the war would be easy. It called on the workers to stop the war by declaring a general strike. The strike call was left out of the St. Louis declaration.

Some of the phrases from Ruthenberg's draft were incorporated in the final product. Attention is called to the following instance. *Ruthenberg wrote*: "In all history there has been no more unjustified war than that which this nation is about to engage in. . . . No greater dishonor has been forced upon a people than that which the capitalist class is forcing upon this nation against its will." *The St. Louis Declaration stated*: "In all modern history there has been no war more unjustifiable than the war in which we are about to engage. No greater dishonor has ever been forced upon a people than that which the capitalist class is forcing upon this nation against its will."

The adoption of the St. Louis Declaration Against War was essentially a Left victory. Such support as it got from Right leaders was half-hearted. Although Berger gave lip-service he took pains to sneer, in the *Milwaukee Leader*,[4] that the Convention which adopted the Declaration was "dominated by the Impossibilist element of the party," meaning, of course, the Left.

Hillquit at first stood firmly on the St. Louis resolution, and, when he ran for mayor of New York City in the Fall, he publicly refused to buy "Liberty" war bonds, even though this country was already in the war. His stand won tremendous popular approval, as expressed by the high vote he received. John F. Hylan, Democrat, won the election with 313,956 votes, and Mayor John P. Mitchell, "good government" candidate, was second with 155,490. Hillquit, on the Socialist ticket, received an unprecedented 145,328 votes, making him a close third—only ten thousand less than second place.[5] Hillquit's anti-war stand won him this increased endorsement. But a month afterward, however, Hillquit—while still professing support for the party's stand—weakened that support in a letter to the *New Republic*.[6] He covered over his anti-war position with conditions and qualifications, adding that the United States was now a belligerent, and, if a referendum were held, he would not vote for withdrawal from the conflict. In another six months his followers on the New York Board of Aldermen were selling as well as buying Liberty Bonds.[7] They also voted, later on, for the temporary Victory Arch on New York's lower Fifth Avenue, which included among the inscriptions commemorating the exploits of the American armies the landings of our soldiers at Murmansk and other Soviet ports—imperialist adventures which were not part of World War I at all but incidents in President Wilson's undeclared war on the young Soviet Republic.

Stand on Conscription

But the Left delegates at St. Louis intended in all seriousness the concrete measures to be taken, including—among others—the following: "Continuous, active, and public opposition to the war, through demonstrations, mass petitions, and all other means within our power. . . . Unyielding opposition to all proposed legislation for military or industrial conscription. Should such conscription be forced upon the people, we pledge ourselves to continuous efforts for the repeal of such laws. . . . Consistent propaganda against military training and militaristic teaching in the public schools."[8]

Cleveland's May Day two weeks later expressed the spirit of

the St. Louis Declaration. The parade was an outpouring of Socialists, trade unionists and sympathizers such as the city had never seen before. And that evening, when Ruthenberg reported on the Convention at Bohemian Gardens, the crowd that packed the hall endorsed the Declaration against the profit-makers' war. At Local Cleveland's convention another fortnight later, on May 13, Ruthenberg was again put up as the Socialist candidate for mayor, and the problem was faced: How oppose war in a country already at war? Since a conscription bill was pending in Congress, the most urgent question was the attitude the party should take if the bill passed. The members decided that, whatever the cost, they must oppose conscription, which they interpreted as "involuntary servitude," a violation of the 13th Amendment. They adopted a resolution against the bill.

At that same meeting a related problem had to be solved: Since the party opposed conscription, should it also oppose *registration for* conscription? Ruthenberg had already made his stand clear. That afternoon he had torn off the wall at party headquarters a leaflet gotten out by a group calling itself the "Young Men's Anti-Militarist League," urging citizens to refuse to register. Despite Ruthenberg's protest, the meeting included in its anti-conscription resolution an appeal to workers to "refuse to register." He was right in objecting to this demand. Refusal to register could only be an individual act of protest against the war. What was needed, as Ruthenberg understood, was organized mass protest. Relying on the constitutional rights of free speech and assembly, he favored large protest meetings and demonstrations. The Conscription Bill, providing for compulsory registration, became a law on May 18, 1917. The Cleveland party, following Ruthenberg's arguments, revoked the "refuse to register" appeal voted the week before, but reaffirmed their stand against conscription. The scheduled anti-conscription meeting was held May 20 as planned.

On May 27, Local Cleveland held another anti-war meeting on the Public Square. As Alfred Wagenknecht, State Secretary, stood up to address the huge crowd, mounted police around the speaker's stand sat sullenly on their horses. As he finished, a federal agent stepped up and arrested him, and the police rode their horses into the crowd, trampling down men and women.

Ruthenberg mounted the rostrum, and the Square became quiet as he began to speak: "My friends and comrades, this is not a war for democracy. This is not a war for freedom. It is not a war for the liberties of mankind. It is a war to secure the investments and the profits of the ruling class of this country. . . . I am speaking to you as Karl Liebknecht spoke in the German nation, as he spoke in the Parliament of that country, when he denounced the war as a war of the ruling class and stated his unalterable opposition to that war. . . . There is no hope for the people . . . unless the people themselves organize their power and make themselves articulate. We can . . . by coming together here, five thousand people this afternoon, and protesting against this conscription law—we can tell the government of this country that we do not want this law and we demand that Congress repeal this law, and . . . if we cannot make this government understand that the people did not want war, that they did not want conscription, then we must await the day until we can go to the election booths again and sweep that government out of power and elect men to power who will represent the wishes of the people . . . and repeal this law, this traitorous act of the ruling class of this country."

"We of the Socialist Party are carrying on this fight," he argued, "that out of the chaos, out of the bloodshed, out of the horror of this war . . . there may come a new society, a new world, a new organization of the people, which will end the cause of war by ending the private ownership of industry which brings war into existence. . . . We are here . . . to end the destruction of millions of lives and billions of wealth, and bring into existence this comradeship of the future, this brotherhood which must inspire the hearts and minds of all men . . . in which for the first time the people will be endowed with those inalienable rights of life, liberty and pursuit of happiness which the Declaration of Independence says are the fundamental rights of every human being. We ask you to work with us to achieve this beautiful goal of Socialism, the brotherhood of man—for today, as never before, rings out in the world the cry of the poet of the social revolution:

"'Come shoulder to shoulder ere the world grows older!
The Cause spreads over land and sea:
Now the earth shaketh, and fear awaketh,
And joy at last for thee and me.'[9]

"Joy at last for me and thee—of the working class—because for the first time there will come into the world this new spirit of love, of equality, fraternity, happiness and peace."[10]

As Ruthenberg stepped down and started for the police station to bail out Wagenknecht, the crowd tried to follow him. Again the mounted police rode them down. At the station Ruthenberg learned that the federal agent and the prosecuting attorney, after a long parley, had charged Wagenknecht simply with "disorderly conduct" and being part of a "disorderly assemblage."

Local Cleveland began circulating a petition to Congress asking repeal of the Conscription Act. The anti-war meetings, at Public Square, Market Square and on the street corners, continued despite growing police persecution. Ruthenberg spoke at nearly every meeting. The city's industrialists and newspapers put pressure on the Printz-Biederman Company to fire Ruthenberg, who was still in their employ. Although this concern had no love for Ruthenberg's ideas or his activities, they did not want to let him go. He was the most efficient office executive and purchasing agent they had ever had.

Daniel Ruthenberg tells how his father was finally discharged. One June day in 1917 his immediate superior, a Mr. Fish, called him in and said he had to choose between the job and his Socialist beliefs. The company made him an exceedingly attractive offer, if he would choose the job. He chose socialism. The story of Ruthenberg's firing has become almost a legend. His brother-in-law Ernst Brandt, with whom he had worked in his teens, tells how he—Brandt—quizzed Ruthenberg about the Printz—Biederman firing.

"I asked him, 'How did it happen, Charley?'" Brandt recalls.

"He told me Mr. Fish says to him, 'Mr. Ruthenberg, if you'll give up the Socialistic Party, we'll give you a block of $10,000 worth of stock outright and a raise in pay to $5,000 a year, and in due time you'll have an opportunity to be a vice-president.' Fish gave him twenty-four hours to make up his mind. But Charley had his mind made up.

"I says to him, 'Charley, will the Socialist Party ever come near that figure for you?' And Charley says, 'It isn't dollars with me, Ernst.'"

It was only after the Printz-Biederman firing that Ruthenberg accepted a salary from the Socialist Party.

Arrest and Trial

But in this same month of June, 1917, a Federal grand jury was meeting secretly in Cleveland to bring indictments against Ruthenberg and his co-workers. Post Office authorities at Washington scrutinized every issue of the *Socialist News.* Secret operatives of the Justice Department prepared to shadow Ruthenberg's movements.

The last week in June, the *Socialist News* was barred from the mails. On Wednesday afternoon, the 27th, Ruthenberg dictated a circular to members of Local Cleveland, announcing the Post Office ban and calling for volunteers to deliver the paper from house to house. He had a speaking engagement the next day in Cincinnati, and hurried home to pack his bag. As he was leaving, the bell rang. Comrades from the office warned that Federal agents had arrested State Secretary Alfred Wagenknecht* and State Organizer Charles Baker, for their speeches of May 20 and May 27, and were coming to get him. Smiling reassuringly, Ruthenberg told his wife Rose to inform the police, if they came, that he had left for Chicago. With that he hurried out the door.

Wagenknecht and Baker were taken to jail, charged with obstructing the Conscription Act. A similar indictment was out against Ruthenberg. A few minutes later the Federal men showed up, and Rose delivered her husband's message. While police contacted Chicago authorities, guards paced all night around the house where Rose and young Daniel were alone.

* On August 26, 1956, Wagenknecht, a founder of the Communist Party, died after a half century of activity on behalf of labor and socialism.

Thursday's newspaper headlines said Ruthenberg had been arrested in Chicago, and locked up in the Fort Sheridan guardhouse. But he was not in Chicago. He had gone to Cincinnati to give his scheduled speech, determined not to disappoint his audience. Returning to Cleveland Friday morning, he went straight to the United States District Attorney's office and announced himself. Chicago police had locked up the wrong man.

Ruthenberg, Wagenknecht and Baker were released on $3,000 bail each. Ruthenberg's brother William was one of his bondsmen. The trial was set for July 16.

The man to whom Ruthenberg had to look for justice at that trial was no stranger to him. As the three defendants walked into the courtroom on the morning of July 16, they faced D. C. Westenhaver, Federal judge of the Northern District of Ohio. Westenhaver was the man who, a few years before, as head of the Cleveland Board of Education, had smashed the attempt to unionize the Cleveland teachers. It was at his order that every teacher who had joined the union had been fired. Westenhaver's anti-labor bias was so well known that the Cleveland Federation of Labor had tried to block his appointment to a judgeship. They even brought pressure on AFL President Samuel Gompers to protest to President Wilson himself against the appointment. But there sat Westenhaver in his judicial robes.

A man whom the defendants did not know from Adam was in the courtroom. He was Alphons J. Schue, the prosecution's star witness, whom Ruthenberg, Wagenknecht and Baker were accused of having persuaded not to register. Schue himself faced a prison term because he had not registered. Defense counsel Joseph W. Sharts, in the course of the trial, described him "as a figure in criminal trials as old as Judas . . . the man who comes in as a confessed criminal in order to clear his own skirts, turn State's evidence, and with the grip of the District Attorney upon his neck, tells what he thinks will serve the purpose and get him free."

Of all the 5,000 people who had listened to the speeches in Public Square on the 20th and the 27th of May, Schue was the only individual the prosecution could find who had been "misled." For, as it developed, Schue claimed it was those speeches in the Square which kept him from registering. Yet even the one police witness who was called was unable to recollect that the three defendants had given any advice whatever in their speeches about registering.

It gradually became clear why the arrests had been postponed a full month after the speeches were delivered. There was no law that forbade speaking against the war or against the Conscription Act. It was illegal only to refuse to register oneself, or to induce others to refuse to register. No one could accuse the defendants of the first, since Baker had registered, and Ruthenberg and Wagenknecht were beyond the age limit. As to proof that the defendants influenced others not to register, that is what the prosecution had combed heaven and earth to find. When they got hold of Schue, as District Attorney Edward S. Wertz admitted in his prosecution speech, "Then the man was unearthed who was influenced" by the speeches in the Square.

The Socialists could expect little understanding from the jury. The Republican Jury Commissioner had picked a venire of Rip Van Winkles to choose the jury from—retired cops and other gentry, ranging in age from 60 to 85. Even these jurors were moved when Ruthenberg, at the request of defense counsel, repeated in court the speech he had delivered May 27 on the Public Square. Prosecutor Wertz, who concentrated his fire on Ruthenberg throughout the trial, was at considerable pains to counteract the effect of the Socialist organizer's eloquence.

He was also at pains to counteract the effect of the obviously friendly attitude of a large part of the audience. Ruthenberg was far from unknown to the people here. He had been born and bred in this very town, and was respected and trusted by his neighbors, by business associates in the firms where he had been employed, by workers in the trade unions he had addressed time and time again. In the courtroom were many who had voted for him for mayor, and would do so again. What was American free speech for, anyhow, they asked themselves at this trial. Prosecutor Wertz was obliged somehow to silence these feelings by a lavish use of patriotic war-mongering. In the end, the verdict was what the Justice Department wanted: "Guilty."

On Wednesday, July 25, 1917, Judge Westenhaver sentenced Ruthenberg, Wagenknecht and Baker to one year in the workhouse at Canton, Ohio. When the prisoners were asked if they had anything to say before sentence was pronounced, Ruthenberg said: "I am not conscious of having committed any crime. The thing I am conscious of is having endeavored to inspire higher ideals and nobler lives. If to do that is a crime in the eyes of the Government, I am proud to have committed that crime."

The three Socialists appealed the verdict, carrying the case straight to the United States Supreme Court. Their defense was backed by Local Cleveland, which undertook to raise a $5,000 defense fund. Out on bail while the appeal was pending, they continued their Socialist activities.

The purpose of the trial of Ruthenberg and his comrades, and of Debs and others soon after, was to shut up all anti-war protest, and to give United States imperialism, then aiming for world hegemony among capitalist nations, a free hand to wage war and achieve the kind of peace it wanted. But the stand Ruthenberg took was an integral part of a long anti-war and anti-imperialist tradition in this country. Only nineteen years earlier the tremendous sentiment against the Spanish-American War, and against the suppression of the independence struggles of the Cuban and Filipino patriots, had led to the setting up in Chicago, October, 1899, of the Anti-Imperialist League, which won the support of Samuel Gompers, who became its vice-president, and of many other labor leaders, along with the backing of such outstanding writers as Mark Twain, William Dean Howells, William James, Edwin Arlington Robinson, Edgar Lee Masters, Dr. W. E. B. Du Bois, Finley Peter Dunne, Carl Schurz, and Thomas Wentworth Higginson.[11]

Ruthenberg was not out of step with American history or with the American people in opposing the war. President Wilson had coined a new slogan, "A War for Democracy," to replace the previous one, "He kept us out of war," but Ruthenberg boldly challenged its truth. Police persecution and the arrest of leaders were a commonplace throughout the country, wherever Socialists raised their voices against the war. In Ohio, besides the three in Cleveland, twenty-four other Socialists were being prosecuted that summer. In the United States as a whole, during the next two years, about a hundred other Socialists were tried before the courts under the so-called espionage law.

The national Socialist leaders who were convicted January 8, 1919, were Victor L. Berger, first Socialist congressman, who was elected again, while his trial was on, against a Republican-Democrat coalition candidate, but barred from taking his seat; Adolph Germer, former national leader of the United Mine Workers who became Socialist national secretary; St. John Tucker, head of the party's lyceum and literature department; J. Louis Engdahl, editor of the *American Socialist,* who later joined the Communist Party and was first editor of the *Daily Worker,* and, still later, head of the International Labor Defense; and William Kruse, head of the Young People's Socialist League. The cases of these five were appealed to the Supreme Court and the verdict reversed, January 31, 1921.

In addition to the Socialists, some 160 members of the Industrial Workers of the World were convicted of conspiracy to obstruct the war effort, and imprisoned for long terms, including Vincent St. John, General Secretary. Several anarchists and hundreds of religious conscientious objectors, most of the latter tried by army court martial because of refusal to serve after being drafted, were similarly sent to prison.

Campaign for Mayor

With a prison sentence hanging over him, Ruthenberg that year waged the greatest Socialist mayoralty campaign in Cleveland's history. Platoons of police surrounded him wherever he spoke, and glowered at the crowd. Federal plainsclothesmen and detectives swarmed through every audience—an old FBI practice.[12] Many of them joined party branches as spies and provocateurs. But thousands of people still flocked to Ruthenberg's weekly meetings in Public and Market Squares.

The tremendous audiences showed how workers felt about the war, throughout the country as well as in Cleveland. The St. Louis Declaration against the War had been ratified in a

Socialist Party referendum by an overwhelming vote. Workers everywhere flocked into the party that summer. In Cleveland, during the six weeks between Ruthenberg's Public Square address and his sentence to prison, 350 new members joined. Ruthenberg's campaign slogan, "For Socialism, Peace and Democracy," penetrated every corner of the city that summer. People saw it and heard it wherever they turned. It was repeated in thousands of leaflets and by dozens of soap-boxers. Party members displayed it on campaign buttons, red ribbon badges, cardboard lapel tags. Clevelanders would get up in the morning and find it on cardboard hangers attached to their doorknobs. Or they would open their mail boxes and find envelopes labeled, "Your Choice," with cards inside showing contrasting programs: in one column, the old-party candidates and the war; in the other, "Vote for Ruthenberg—for Socialism, Peace and Democracy."

When Mrs. Yetta Land, a family friend of Ruthenberg, took him to his speaking assignments in her car, her four-year-old son Sanford often rode in the back seat. Little Sandy, who was to grow up to fight for democracy in Spain, took a great interest in the speaking. One afternoon Sandy came running across the street from his play, clutching something in his hands. "Gi' me a hat quick!" he told his mother. Into the hat he poured pennies, panting "Made a collection for my speech!"

"Why, what on earth did he say?" the puzzled mother asked a neighbor.

"He told us," said the neighbor, "Comrades and friends, we are here tonight to bring you a message of Socialism, Peace and Democracy!"

Labor Day, 1917, was bright and beautiful. Thousands headed for the Cleveland Federation of Labor's annual picnic at Luna Park, looking forward to the traditional forum for mayoralty candidates. All five candidates were there. Ruthenberg spoke last. While the first four speakers were talking, hundreds strolled about in the grounds nearby. As the evening wore on, people in the audience began to shout for Ruthenberg. When he got up to talk, the strollers swarmed back into the auditorium, jamming every corner. People filled the window sills, and climbed trees outside to lean and listen. The audience of at least 10,000 shouted and stamped their approval as Ruthenberg denounced the war and the Conscription Act.

Suddenly Republican Mayor Harry L. Davis began edging quietly off the platform. A moment later, a group of soldiers pushed their way into the hall. The disrupters lurched close to the platform, and drunken cursing voices demanded that Ruthenberg stop talking. He held his ground. The rowdies piled up on the platform, knocking down and beating those in their way. Federation of Labor officials remonstrated in vain. Democratic candidate William S. Stinchcomb got socked in the eye. The meeting was broken up. Thousands rushed for the exits, while a number of stout-hearted workers fought back against the goons.

It was exactly half-past nine that the soldiers had entered the hall. Fifteen minutes later, as the crowd poured into the street, newsboys were already selling a special edition of the *Plain Dealer* telling about the Luna Park "riot." Charges that the riot had been staged, with the connivance of Mayor Davis and the press, were never effectively denied. The thugs had gone there to get Ruthenberg, but could not find him. Rose and twelve-year-old Daniel were looking for him, too, and Rose was worried. When she and Daniel finally got home, they found Ruthenberg waiting for them, leaning back in an easy chair perusing the *Plain Dealer*. He explained, smiling, that the vaudeville entertainers, who were waiting in the wings to put on an act after his speech, had yanked him out of sight into their dressing room. Then he went out the stage door with the entertainers and got home ahead of everybody.

The provocation at Luna Park backfired. Indignation swept the city. The Cleveland Federation of Labor sent an angry resolution of protest to the Secretary of War, Baker, who replied with a promise to "investigate" the soldiers' part in the riot. Ruthenberg also sent a letter to Baker, recalling that in 1911, when the Secretary of War was himself a candidate for mayor, Baker and Ruthenberg had shared the Luna Park platform on Labor Day. The rioting soldiers, Ruthenberg urged, should receive prompt punishment to show "That the Constitutional rights of free speech and free assemblage still exist in this country."

The tremendous popular support Ruthenberg got that autumn did not halt surveillance by the police. They never ceased to dog his footsteps. Daniel recalls how police and detectives used to come to the house, banging on the door at all hours of the night. They made frequent searches, peering and prying into every corner from attic to basement.

"One time," Daniel says, "they searched my playroom and found what I thought was a swell and authentic Mechano replica of a submarine. They lugged it off with them, apparently taking it for some infernal instrument."

But police or no police, people kept talking about Ruthenberg. Straw votes in shops began to show him as first choice for mayor. In street-corner polls, he ran second, or at least third. Liberal churches invited him to address their forums, despite the fact that he had been sentenced to prison. Reverend Herbert S. Bigelow of Cincinnati, speaking in Cleveland, advised citizens to vote for Ruthenberg. The worried Civic League, however, issued a special bulletin urging the defeat of the Socialist candidate.

The newspapers, willy-nilly, were impressed. At least one Cleveland daily prepared an advance story, in case the Socialist candidate should be successful. A yellowed galley proof of this quarter-column item, marked "Hold for Release," has been preserved. It begins, "Cleveland's mayor-elect is under sentence to a year in the workhouse," and continues with a polite newspaper-style biography. While he was not elected, he got a phenomenal vote. He ran a strong third, receiving 27,685 votes, more than twice what he had gotten in 1915. His campaign swept three other Socialists into office: Noah Mandelkorn and John G. Willert as councilmen and A. L. Hitchcock as a member of the Board of Education.

8

FROM CANTON PRISON—A NEW VISTA

THAT SUMMER and autumn of 1917, while the appeal to the Supreme Court was pending, Ruthenberg began to learn from Lenin, as he had previously learned from Marx. Wartime reaction had worsened, and new problems faced him as a Socialist organizer, but he found time—he *had* to have time—to ponder the intensely exciting developments in Russia. It was not just the revolution of the previous March, which ended tsarism: there was a revolution a-borning *within* that revolution, and the stirring Bolshevik slogan, "All power to the Soviets," echoed across the Atlantic. The "Soviets" or *Councils* were composed of representatives of ordinary people, elected at public meetings. There were Soviets of workers in the factories, of peasants in the villages, of soldiers in the army, of sailors in the navy. And from these rank and file Soviets delegates were elected to the All-Russian Congress of Soviets. "Power" to *them* would mean working class control of the state, and control under Bolshevik leadership would mean a chance to build socialism.

There was a steady increase of Bolshevik influence in Russia, and a grand rise in socialist prestige throughout the world. What the collapse of the Second International had destroyed, the growth of Bolshevism had restored: working class confidence in the future. Ruthenberg recalled how, eight years before, he had begun to study Marx. Up to that time he had looked upon the ideas of Paine and Jefferson as the most enlightened in history. Then, in reading Marx, he had seen socialism at first as an enlightened enlargement and carrying forward of the ideas of the Declaration of Independence and the Rights of Man, and, later, as a raising of these concepts of liberty, equality and brotherhood to a new level, a higher democracy, embracing economic as well as political freedom for the great mass of the people. Now Lenin's Bolshevism came to him, quite clearly, as an enlightened carrying forward of Marxism, under the conditions of his time and country. Lenin faced the problems of the immediate struggle in Russia at the same time that he saw further into the future than William Morris' *News from Nowhere,* the famous novel of utopian communism. What particularly struck Ruthenberg was Lenin's leadership in immediately carrying forward the bourgeois democratic revolution, won in March, into the proletarian socialist revolution.

Up to this year, Ruthenberg had ascertained next to nothing of Lenin. It was not until after the Revolution in March, 1917, when Lenin returned from exile, that news about him crept into the American press. Ruthenberg got his first authentic information about Lenin's work as early as April, when a Russian-born Socialist named Boris Reinstein, who years before had joined the old Socialist Labor Party, lectured in Cleveland on the history of the Socialist movement in Russia, culminating in the overthrow of the Tsar.[1] That same month a dispatch in the New York *Times* from Petrograd (now Leningrad) told how a Bolshevik crowd protested before the American embassy about Tom Mooney, principal in a labor defense case in the American courts at that time, which American Socialists were much concerned about. The dispatch blamed Lenin for the anti-American demonstration.[2] Mooney, an American labor leader and Socialist, had been framed at the time of the military preparedness parade in San Francisco, July 22, 1916, when a bomb had been thrown, and was under sentence of death. Ambassador David R. Francis, who had never heard of Mooney, cabled on inquiry to President Wilson. It was Wilson's subsequent telegram to Governor Hiram W. Johnson of California that led to commuting Mooney's sentence to life imprisonment. Some twenty years later—after a generation of struggle on his behalf—Mooney was set free. In May, 1917, American correspondents in Russia reported that "At the present time, one name is on everybody's lips—Lenin."[3] All that summer, his stirring appeals to the Russian soldiers and sailors appeared regularly in the New York *Call.* Lenin's following, though still a minority party, was rapidly gaining adherents in the local and All-Russian Soviets, and, here in the United States, Ruthenberg felt that Lenin's ideas about immediate peace and a workers' government were sound. As early as June, 1917, at a meeting in Market Square, he praised the demand for peace which was being pushed by Bolshevik deputies at sessions of the Workers' and Soldiers' Councils.

The November Revolution

Then came the magnificent Socialist Revolution itself, on November 7, led by Lenin and the Bolsheviks. The fight of the Russian workers for democratic rights and an end to tsarism had heightened into the successful socialist revolution. A new age was starting—a new era for all humankind.

An overjoyed Ruthenberg drew up a greeting to the triumphant Russian workers, pledging support to their revolution, and calling an emergency convention of Local Cleveland to hail the event. Ruthenberg was particularly elated that the first act of the Russian Councils of Workers and Soldiers, after seizure of power, was to call for an end of the war. When the convention met, Ruthenberg's greeting to the new Socialist revolution was adopted officially and distributed throughout the city a few days later in leaflet form. "The effort of the Bolsheviks to establish peace," the resolution proclaimed, "through the action of the workers of all countries, a peace not based upon the interests of the ruling classes of the nations involved nor attained through the trading of diplomats, but based upon the interests of the workers and established through the aggressive action of the workers, a peace without annexations and without indemnities, offers the only hope of saving our civilization from destruction. In this effort we pledge to the workers of Russia our earnest support. We hail the policy of their present government as the true expression of proletarian action, and pledge ourselves to do all in our power to assist in wiping out capitalist imperialism and in establishing the civilization of the future, the commonwealth of the workers united irrespective of nationality."

Ruthenberg was convinced that the Bolsheviks were the true Marxists of Russia, and that much could be learned from a study of their theoretical writings and from their experience. About the time of the Bolshevik uprising, he read—aside from news items about Lenin and occasional quotations ascribed to him—an article by Lenin himself which set him to thinking. It was "Political Parties in Russia," which appeared in translation in the new Left Wing magazine, *Class Struggle,* published in New York. He eagerly read translations of other political articles from the Russian, some of which appeared in *The Internationalist,* a periodical published in Boston by the Lettish Socialist Federation.

He read avidly about the Russian Revolution, both before he entered prison in late January, 1918, and after he got out in December of the same year. "The Bolsheviks . . . are the foes of every kind of imperialism," he wrote on January 12, 1918, in the *Socialist News.* "They stand for a new kind of world." The test of a socialist, he thought, is how much he wants that new kind of world! In the spring of 1917, the key issue in the United States had been opposition to the imperialist war. After the fall of 1917, as soon as the Socialist Revolution occurred, the attitude toward it became the test of socialist convictions. But the pledge of solidarity that Local Cleveland made to the Russian workers was outstanding. Not everywhere was there full support among Socialists for the Bolsheviks. In Toledo, Left Wing Socialists and members of the Young People's Socialist League wanted to follow Cleveland's example, but were threatened with expulsion by the local Right leadership. Ruthenberg hurried to Toledo. He explained to the membership, as old-timers there still recall, that the world's first successful socialist revolution had taken place in Russia, and it was up to real socialists all over the world to support it.

Day by day, as the Supreme Court moved through its calendar of cases, Ruthenberg—uncertain whether or not he would go to prison—hastened to reach the people. "Faster! Faster!" he urged in the *Socialist News.* He strove to spread quickly throughout Cleveland and Ohio the news of what had really happened in Russia. "There never was a greater emergency than the present," he wrote, early in January. "Things are moving fast in the world. Governments and thrones are rocking. . . . The Socialist movement the world over is wielding more power than ever before in its history. The future belongs to the workers. . . . Our task is to build the working class movement in Cleveland."

In Cleveland, he said. The job nearest at hand, in his own bailiwick! He became a national and even international figure as organizer of Local Cleveland.

Canton Workhouse

Then on January 14 the message came. The Supreme Court had upheld the conviction of the Ohio Socialists, sentenced to serve a year in the Canton Workhouse. And the following Sunday, January 20, in a heavy snowfall, three thousand people came to icy Market Square to say good-bye to Ruthenberg and his co-workers, soon to be taken to Canton.

"Our message to the workers may be silenced," Ruthenberg told the sober-faced crowd, "but that message should be taken up by earnest men and women and brought home to the people of this city. . . . In a year from now we shall return . . . to take up the work for the cause we have fought for and for which we will again fight—the cause of Socialism, Peace and Democracy, which before many more months go by will sweep over the world and triumph everywhere."

Late Thursday afternoon, January 31, 1918, a little group of men and women emerged from Cleveland's Federal Building and headed for the County Jail a short distance away. Newspaper cameras clicked, and reporters followed along. At the head of the group strode Ruthenberg. Behind him walked Wagenknecht and a United States marshall. In the rear came Marguerite Prevey, Socialist leader from Akron, and Wagenknecht's wife Hortense. Ruthenberg and Wagenknecht were being taken to the jail to join Baker, who was already there. The next morning the three prisoners would be taken to the

Workhouse at Canton, Ohio, to start serving their terms.

As the group approached the jail, newspapermen taunted Ruthenberg with the question, what would happen to the Socialist Party, with the leaders locked up. The leaders' wives, Ruthenberg assured the reporters, would be among those who would carry on the work. A few minutes later, the doors of the County Jail closed behind the prisoners. Marguerite Prevey and Hortense Wagenknecht walked up the street alone, on their way to join Rose Ruthenberg, who was waiting for them at the Socialist Party headquarters, 737 Prospect Avenue.

Rose was the first of the "earnest men and women" who, as her husband had predicted, stepped forward to take the place of the imprisoned leaders. She took charge of Local Cleveland's office, became a member of the City Central Committee, and received his modest salary until he was released. Young Harry Checel handled the organizing work; veteran Tom Clifford edited the *Socialist News*. At the State Office in nearby Lakewood, Hortense Wagenknecht carried on in her husband's place.

Cleveland's capitalist press jeered that Ruthenberg and his comrades were "trying on their new striped suits." Within a week sneering stories told of a "regimen of bread and water," and described the Socialists as toiling at the prison's laundry. There were dark hints that other ways had been found to tame these men. The Socialists of Cleveland were oppressed by a growing uneasiness. Then, at Akron, Marguerite Prevey received a strange visitor, a prisoner just released from Canton, who told her that Ruthenberg and Wagenknecht were being tortured.

Mrs. Prevey quickly got in touch with party leaders, and a delegation rushed to Canton. They took with them Attorney Morris Herbert Wolf, who had been associated with Joseph H. Sharts in the defense of the three. Going directly to the Workhouse supervisor, they insisted on seeing the prisoners at once. The supervisor refused. On the basis of the grapevine information that had come to the party, Wolf and others accused the supervisor point blank of secretly torturing the Socialist leaders in the prison's dreaded dark "hole." They threatened an exposé in the Cleveland newspapers of the medieval brutalities that went on there. The supervisor retreated. He tried to cover himself by saying that Ruthenberg had been "impudent," and had tried to "run the jail." He had Baker and Wagenknecht and finally Ruthenberg, called to the office, and allowed Wolf, in his capacity of attorney, to see them. Ruthenberg had to be helped into the room by the prison guards. He was so weak he could hardly stand, but his eyes were hot with rage. He collapsed in a chair. He had just been brought from the "hole."

Wagenknecht's story of what happened in those first prison days is as follows: After several days in separate cells, the three were assigned to work—Baker to the kitchen, Ruthenberg and himself to the laundry. The first morning, Wagenknecht got down to the laundry a moment later than Ruthenberg, and found him rebelling against the foul job of scrubbing prison clothes by hand in the stinking steam-laden cellar. Ruthenberg was telling the Workhouse captain in no uncertain terms that he would not work there. Wagenknecht immediately backed him up.

The supervisor ordered Ruthenberg to the "hole," a black and windowless isolation cell. There he was strung up by the wrists, with his toes barely touching the floor, for ten hours, without either water or food. Wagenknecht was chained to his cell door. The next morning both men again refused to work in the laundry. This time, Wagenknecht was taken to the "hole" and Ruthenberg chained to his cell door. The third day—the day the Socialist delegation came to the rescue—Ruthenberg was once more strung up in the "hole." When he was brought to the prison office, the guards had just unlocked the handcuffs by which he had already been hanging for several hours. The prison supervisor, caught red-handed, had to negotiate. It was finally agreed that Ruthenberg and Wagenknecht would work in the laundry for one day, after which they would receive other assignments.

From now on, Ruthenberg and Wagenknecht had better treatment. They were soon put at outdoor work, hired out to farmers for whom they did everything from cutting grass to hoeing cabbage. One farmer reduced their duties to a minimum, and looked the other way when they held a picnic under the open sky. It was not long till the prison authorities discovered Ruthenberg's gifts for clerical work, and put him to work in the prison office. Wagenknecht tells how he and Ruthenberg began cautiously to build for themselves, even behind the bars at Canton, a bearable life, to prepare themselves for the future. They now shared the same cell. Wagenknecht, who still worked on the farm, smuggled in apples, slipped up his sleeve, and they would have "banquets" of apples and white bread. They played checkers, and quietly talked politics.

Every visiting day, Rose Ruthenberg, Hortense Wagenknecht and the faithful party worker Ann Morgan came to see them and bring them papers and other literature. On Memorial Day (April 30) there was a mass visit, with some twenty-five automobiles, loaded with people, lined up before the Workhouse. Rose told her husband of Daniel's progress in school, and, as well as she could, the news that wasn't in the newspapers he was allowed to read. She memorized summaries of important items, repeated messages from friends and comrades, received suggestions from him about pressing problems faced in the office. She told him, among other things, how the two Socialist Councilmen, Mandelkorn and Willert, elected the previous fall, had been ousted from the Cleveland City Council, and how Hitchcock, Socialist member of the Cleveland Board of Education, had been sent to Atlanta Penitentiary under the new espionage law. She told him, too, about other Ohio Socialists jailed for anti-war activity, including his friends in Cincinnati, Lotta Burke and Thomas Hammerschmidt.[4]

Soon Ruthenberg began to write. He managed to get paper from the prison office. At first it was impossible to get any of his articles out of the Workhouse. But later the three women visitors were watched less closely. Ruthenberg's first article from prison, "On the Threshold of the New World," appeared under the initials "C.E.R." in the *Socialist News* of April 27, 1918, just in time for May Day. He sought to dispel despondency by this May Day message. Behind prison bars, he was able to point to new doors opening for the working class.

"There are those in our movement," he wrote, "who view

our present situation through blue goggles. The unabated fury of the war, the frenzy created by the interested capitalist papers resulting in rioting . . . the prosecution of many comrades under the Espionage Act . . . these things, they believe, make effective continuance of our propaganda impossible. That is a false notion."

He added: "In counting our gains and losses . . . we must not overlook the splendid service which the Bolsheviks have rendered. Although their consistent and courageous stand has been twisted and distorted in the reports of the capitalist press, millions of working men have been reached by the message of International Working Class Solidarity."

He undertsood very well indeed that what made the world different was the Bolshevik Revolution in Russia. And he understood its need for peace, for rebuilding industry and building socialism. A later article, published on May 25—though it revealed how sketchy was the information available to him—boldly championed the Brest-Litovsk Peace with Germany, which took Soviet Russia out of the imperialist war.

The Imprisonment of Debs

On June 16, 1918, came the famed Socialist Party State Convention and picnic at Canton, when Debs gave the speech that sent him to Atlanta Penitentiary.[5] The picnic, held in conjunction with the Convention, took place, as planned, in Nimisilla Park, across the street from the Workhouse, so that Ruthenberg and his comrades might look and listen—a little—from their cell windows. Thousands of people, as well as delegates to the Convention, attended the outing. Before going to the Convention, Debs visited his friends in the Workhouse, and was able to talk personally to Ruthenberg, by whom he sent greetings to Baker and Wagenknecht. At the Convention in a nearby hall he spoke out good and strong, clearly inspired by the steadfast courage of the imprisoned Socialists.

"I have just returned from a visit over yonder," he said, pointing toward the Workhouse as the delegates cheered, "where three of our most loyal comrades are paying the penalty for their devotion to the cause of the working class. They have come to realize, as many of us have, that it is extremely dangerous to exercise the constitutional right of free speech in a country fighting to make democracy safe for the world. . . . Those boys over yonder, those comrades of ours—and how I love them—aye, they are our younger brothers, their names are seared in our souls."

The crowd applauded again when Debs turned to the subject of the Russian Revolution of the previous autumn, November 7, 1917. "Here, in this assemblage I hear our heart beat responsive to the Bolsheviks of Russia. Yes, those heroic men and women, those unconquerable comrades, who have, by their sacrifice, added fresh lustre to the international movement. . . . The first act of that immortal revolution was to proclaim a state of peace with all the world, coupled with an appeal, not to the kings, not to the emperors, not to the rulers, not to the diplomats, but an appeal to the people of all nations. . . ." Then he said: "Yes, in good time we are going to sweep into power in this nation and throughout the world. . . . The world is daily changing before our eyes. The sun of capitalism is setting; the sun of Socialism is rising. It is our duty to build the new nation and the free republic."

Later in the summer, after he had been indicted for what he said at Canton, Debs gave the same speech again, in an expanded and even more militant form, at a national Socialist conference in Chicago. He made it clear that he meant what he said. He was arrested for the Canton speech, tried under the Espionage Act, and sentenced at the Cleveland federal court, September 14, 1918, to ten years in prison. Sentence was pronounced by the same Judge Westenhaver who had sent Ruthenberg, Wagenknecht and Baker to the Workhouse.

The Debs trial, the futile appeal to the Supreme Court, and his subsequent imprisonment, first at Moundsville, W. Va., Prison and then at Atlanta Federal Penitentiary, aroused the whole world. Debs conducted his own defense, though a battery of lawyers headed by Seymour Steadman was at his side. He relied on the plain meaning of the First Amendment to the Constitution, which guarantees freedom of speech, press and assembly. He denied that he ever advocated violence, declared that he always appealed to the reason and conscience of the people. He praised the Bolsheviks of Russia, and proclaimed his support of socialism everywhere. "I am not on trial here," he said, in his final two-hour address to the jury. "There is an infinitely greater issue that is being tried in this country, though you may not be conscious of it. American institutions are on trial here before a court of American citizens. . . ."[6]

Debs' conviction climaxed the summer when women picketed Woodrow Wilson in Washington, demanding the vote, and Carl Sandburg in the New York *Call* described the white terror in Finland which drowned in blood the young Finnish Soviet Republic. It was the summer that a hundred odd leading members of the IWW were railroaded to jail for "conspiracy," and Victor Berger and four staff members of the Socialist National Executive Committee were put on trial for support of the St. Louis anti-war resolution. In Cleveland, the *Socialist News* reported the arrest there of the Negro Socialist writers, A. Phillips Randolph and Chandler Owen, for street-corner speaking. John Reed, war correspondent and labor journalist, already known to Socialists for his reporting of the Mexican revolution, and who had just seen the Socialist Revolution in Russia, spoke in Cleveland's Gray's Armory and in halls of other cities after his return to this country. He lectured on the topic, "The Truth About Russia," and voiced the demand, "Recognize Russia." His great book, *Ten Days That Shook the World,* came out shortly afterward and immediately became world famous.[7]

"After the War—What?"

Doggedly facing persecution, Cleveland Socialists kept going. Rose Ruthenberg was for the first time a delegate to the state convention and to state party meetings. Nomination petitions for the fall elections put Ruthenberg's name on the ballot for Congress. In prison, he got 4,724 votes.

In the *Socialist News* of November 23, 1918, appeared the

modest announcement that "Cleveland Socialists and their friends will welcome the three men [Ruthenberg, Wagenknecht, and Baker] at a great mass meeting to be held at Acme Hall, 2416 E. 9th St., on Sunday, Dec. 15, at 2:30 in the afternoon." The men had been released on Monday, December 3, after serving ten months. A few friends, including Gene Debs himself, Marguerite Prevey, and of course Rose Ruthenberg and Hortense Wagenknecht, took them from the Workhouse to the home of a sympathizer, where they had a "liberation breakfast" and talked and talked.

They were free, but there was work to do. Ruthenberg inwardly gazed at the road of struggle ahead. Even as he laughed and talked, he was thinking and planning.

Twelve days later he addressed a packed crowd of Clevelanders at the Welcome Home mass meeting in Acme Hall. "As I stand here facing you," he said, "with the open portals of a prison not far behind me, I hurl into the faces of the rulers of society the same defiance that all the prisons on the face of the earth cannot break the spirit of men and women who have in their hearts the hope and inspiration which the Socialist movement gives."

The issue of the *Socialist News* which announced the Welcome Home mass meeting also promised a series of articles under the title, "After the War—What?" No by-line was given, but when the series begun two weeks later, Ruthenberg's name was down as the author.[8] In the ten installments of the series Ruthenberg presented the Socialist argument in a fresh way—the changes that were necessary in the world, the lessons of wartime control of industry, the dangers faced by organized labor, the "road to freedom." The final articles, dealing with "The End of War" and "Servile State or Socialism," were prophetic. He pointed out that the slogan of "a war to end war" was illusory, that there was nothing in the League of Nations (then being formed) to prevent future war because the capitalist battle for markets and profits kept on going. And he warned that the winning of socialism was the only safeguard against the iron heel of a threatening "industrial feudalism."

The new plans he had thought about in prison were put

into motion in those first days: First came the Reconstruction Organization Campaign, as he called it. "Every reader of the *Socialist News,*" he wrote, "will receive an invitation to help in this Reconstruction Organization Campaign during the next few days. . . . Act quickly." Second was the fight for "Amnesty for Political Prisoners," launched in the party paper on December 28 and followed up with impassioned mass rallies. Third was a determined effort to build the circulation of the *Socialist News* from 7,500 to double that number. Fourth was his firm resolve to go personally to the people, starting with a series of four Sunday evening lectures, and clarify the significance of Soviet Russia and the international issues its existence underlined. The Russian workers were starting to build a socialist state, and Socialists in other countries must be alert, he reasoned, to study the plans of the Bolsheviks and give them whatever help they could. The talks would be limited to fifty minutes, it was specified, "to be followed by forty minutes of questions and discussion from the audience." As these meetings got under way, he gave out-of-town lectures on "real socialism," beginning January 3, in Youngstown, Columbus, Toledo, Akron, Sandusky and Lorain.

As the year 1919 began, Ruthenberg got out a signed leaflet headed "Forward! March!" to speed the building of the *Socialist News* circulation. "As long as the capitalist class controls the source through which the workers get their information, it will be impossible to overthrow capitalism," he said. He explained that it was necessary to get around the power wielded by the capitalist class through its management and ownership of the commercial press. To break "capitalist control over the minds of the workers" was "the big task," he stressed.

It was at this time that he read Lenin's *A Letter to American Workers.* It was like a personal message from the great Marxist leader whom he had been thinking about during the months he had spent in prison. In this *Letter* the man who had led the socialist revolution the preceding autumn revealed himself as nearby in spirit, thinking warmly of American workers, talking directly to them, familiar with their history, sympathetic with their problems. Ruthenberg read it in the December, 1918, issue of the New York *Class Struggle,* and later the same month (December 22, 1918) saw it again in the Boston *Revolutionary Age.* The powerful logic of Lenin's *Letter* reached thousands of American Socialists throughout the country.[9]

Lenin sought to explain to American workers the meaning of the socialist revolution that had taken place in Russia, particularly since the United States Government was intervening against it more and more, even sending armed soldiers in an attempt to forcibly overthrow the newly established Soviet government. The United States was in fact one of a dozen governments—including France, England, Japan—which were at this time not only supplying arms to whitegard tsarist generals but sending in troops of their own in an effort to halt the building of socialism. Lenin reminded Americans of their own "great, really liberating, really revolutionary" War of Independence. "The American people," he wrote, "gave the world an example of a revolutionary war against feudal subjection." Today, however, the descendants of those Americans, he said, were in in a new kind of subjection, in a state of wage slavery to a handful of capitalist billionaires. The Russian workers had won a revolution against this kind of wage slavery, and American workers should uphold the right of Russian workers to the fruits of *their* revolution.

The vista of Socialism for the United States, which Ruthenberg beheld with an inner eye as he emerged from prison, was confirmed and illuminated by the clarity and the fervor of Lenin's *Letter.* The Bolsheviks had reached the workers and peasants of Russia with the message of peace and socialism, and there came about, he saw, the most democratic revolution of all history. Couldn't American workers and farmers also be reached with the message of socialism, a message so much in accord with the *common sense* of our Revolutionary War and the All-men-are-born-free-and-equal of our Declaration of Independence? Of course they could! Let the *real socialists* of this country get to work!

9

SOCIALIST TO COMMUNIST

RUTHENBERG SAW early in 1919, and more and more as events developed, that the old type of Socialist Party leaders—here as well as abroad—were not the men to build a new world. That a new world was being built, and needed the help of all Socialists of good will, was as clear as day. He himself was resolved to shove with all his might toward the future. In mid-January the Ohio *Socialist* carried the complete text of the new Soviet constitution. And before the month was out the Cleveland *Socialist News* (which carried his article, "The Bolsheviks: Grave-Diggers of Capitalism") announced that Locals Cleveland, Boston and Portland had petitioned the National Executive Committee for a special convention on affiliation with the Bolshevik-sponsored new international organization which was being discussed but had not yet been formed.

In February, when the newly formed Left Wing Section of the Socialist Party of New York published its *Left Wing Manifesto and Program,* Ruthenberg at once recognized its importance. The Ohio *Socialist* re-printed it on February 26, and the Cleveland *Socialist News* on March 1. It was the first complete declaration of principles gotten out by the Left, and it was adopted by local after local, state after state, as the tentative program of the entire Left wing of the Socialist Party. While the war was on, the exodus of Right-wingers into the ranks of the war-mongers had been so startling as to make the whole Right suspect, even though their other weaknesses were overlooked. But they could not be overlooked. It could not be forgotten that the Socialist Party, under the leadership of Hillquit and other Centrists, tried to resurrect the old Second International which had passed away and been entombed at the start of the War. These leaders shied away from all efforts by Lenin and others, before 1917, to establish a new international organization which might be kept free from the opportunists. Instead, as Ruthenberg saw with astonished disgust, Hillquit's group chose delegates to a so-called "middle-of-the-road" Stockholm conference which never met at all. And after 1917, when the Socialist Revolution was won and growing, the Hillquit group dawdled on the question of supporting it, issuing statements of hesitant "endorsement" of the Soviets as a kind of delaying tactics in their secret war on the Left.

In addition to the old issues on which the Left opposed the Right leadership, there were these new issues: support to the new Soviet Republic, opposition to the United States military intervention against it, and affiliation to the newly formed Communist International, issues which Ruthenberg believed of the most vital importance to the working class of this and of every other country. The Hillquit group which held Socialist Party leadership toyed with these matters, afraid to withhold approval because of the vigorous rank and file support for the Bosheviks; but determined, nonetheless, never to commit the Socialist Party to any course of action that would be a serious threat to American imperialism. Under these circumstances, with these national problems and issues racing toward an early—perhaps a too early—solution, May Day, 1919, approached in Cleveland, a May Day destined to be historic. Debs' appeal to the Supreme Court was over, and he was taken to prison. Ruthenberg organized 19 street protest meetings in Cleveland, and spoke at five of them, in the last days before the old leader was jailed. The day after Debs was taken to prison, Ruthenberg led a protest parade to Public Square. On April 26 his editorial demanded: "Open the Prison Doors."

The May Day Parade

The gigantic May Day celebration in Cleveland was designed to stress Ruthenberg's new campaign for mayor, and his program for working class progress. The war was over, but capitalism's post-war assault on labor was already launched. The workers, Ruthenberg saw, must learn the happy truth about the Socialist triumphs abroad, and protect themselves against the new employer-planned anti-labor drive at home. Among the speakers he had brought to Ohio to lecture on events abroad was Colonel Raymond Robbins, head of the American Red Cross in Russia, who exposed the lie that Lenin was a German agent. Another was Santeri Nuorteva, originally an editor of a Finnish Socialist paper and later a representative of the Finnish workers' republic, who showed how the Socialist regime in his country had been crushed by the Finnish white terror assisted—*with Allied approval*—by the German army. These first-hand reports on various facets of capitalist duplicity served to speed Ruthenberg's own education, too. They helped him understand the ugly face American imperialism showed—and would show—to workers right here in democratic America.

May Day was bright and sunny, and the parade was a gala affair. Thirty branches of Local Cleveland marched with trade unionists and sympathizers in four columns, carrying banners and placards, to Public Square.[1] One hundred thousand gaily dressed men, women and children were in the parade or on the sidelines, singing, cheering, laughing. A number of marchers were in Army uniform. Placards demanded freedom for Debs and Mooney, withdrawal of American troops from Soviet Russia, help for the unemployed, "Workers of the World, Unite!" The first column, headed by Ruthenberg, rolled into the Square, and the throng already gathered there gave them a welcoming cheer.

Then the attack began. Mounted police galloped into the line, swinging their clubs. Army tanks and trucks rolled upon the marchers. Autos drove up carrying police and "Loyal American League" members, and all of them wielded clubs. Every red rose or necktie, every red waist worn by a woman, they tore off and trampled. Men, women and children broke and ran, fleeing into alleys where they were still pursued. Men fought back with bare fists, or with the staffs that held their placards.

"I saw a peaceable line of unarmed paraders attacked on an obviously preconcerted signal," wrote Ted Robinson, reporter for the Cleveland *Plain Dealer*, years afterward. "I saw men and women brutally beaten. . . . I saw the blood flow in sickening streams at the city's busiest corner; I saw the victims arrested while the attackers went free; and I saw the fining and jailing of these victims on the following day." The mayor well knew that the parade would be attacked, Robinson added, but he did nothing about it.

Two people were killed, scores injured. Ruthenberg was arrested and charged with "Assault with intent to kill," and released on bail. Doubtless those who *charged* Ruthenberg with murder hoped he would *be* murdered. Old timers recall threats against his life: groups were organized to guard his home. "We kept up the guard night and day, in shifts, for several weeks after May Day," says one who was himself a guard.

Acting with his usual energy, Ruthenberg got out a leaflet offering $500 reward for information leading to the punishment "of the person or persons who organized the attacks upon the Socialist May Day parade." The leaflet insisted that the Socialists were within their legal rights in marching through the streets, yet the police, instead of arresting the hoodlums, "aided them" in beating Socialists. It asked questions: "Where was the meeting held on Wednesday night preceding the May Day parade, at which the hoodlums and gangsters were organized to beat up the Socialists? Who are the discharged soldiers who have been boasting about the wads of money they got as a result of their help in smashing the May Day parade? Who paid them? Who drove the truck which brought a load of automobile spokes from an East End factory, which were later used in the attack upon the Socialists?[2] Who drove the truck that stood before the Hotel Cleveland, from which baseball bats were distributed with instructions to 'help kill the Bolsheviks'? What was the license number?"

Another leaflet followed, entitled "Who Are the Murderers?" It ridiculed the capitalist press about the supposed "Bolshevik uprising" that had been "put down." There was "no trouble along the line of march, miles long," the leaflet said, until they got to the Square. Working people who lined the streets showed no disapproval: they applauded. There were no police along those streets to "maintain order"! "It is true that the Socialists carried the red flag," the leaflet said. "There is no law against carrying the red flag." It charged that Cleveland newspapers lied when they reported that Ruthenberg promised no red flags would be carried. On the contrary: "Police Captain Granel called at Ruthenberg's home Wednesday night and was given a typewritten outline of the line of march and the complete plan of the Socialists for the demonstration. He asked about the red flag and was told that it would be carried in the parade because May Day and the red flag stood for the same ideal—the brotherhood of man."

In a letter, May 15, 1919, to the New York *Communist,* Left wing organ edited by John Reed, Ruthenberg said the ruling class was "trying to railroad Tom Clifford [local Socialist organizer] and me to the penitentiary for from one to fifteen years." He added: "We have about a hundred comrades in the workhouse; most of them, in addition to their days [of imprisonment] have a fine included in their sentence, and we must raise $2,500 to pay those fines so they will not have to work them out at sixty cents a day." He concluded: "Last night we accepted 355 new members."

The May Day outrage boomeranged against the plotters. The mob attack had taken place directly in front of the Hotel Cleveland, where the Inter-Faith World Conference was meeting, and delegates had watched from the windows. One of them, Rev. Worth M. Tippy, stated flatly that the Socialists "did not cause the riots."[3]

The *Plain Dealer* reported on June 11 that officially it was Patrolmen Charles Kern and Frank Zika who had brought the "Assault to kill" charge against Ruthenberg. Half-a-year later, December 3, it mentioned, as though in an aside, that he had been freed by Judge Dan Cull because the case was "nolled." Though a murder trial against Ruthenberg had been scheduled, no jury was impaneled, no witnesses called, no court proceedings held. The prosecutor simply "moved to dismiss," and that was all.

The Split

These May Day events in Cleveland—the violent assaults on the workers and the heroic Socialist resistance under Ruthenberg's leadership—aroused the Left forces of the entire country, and served as a significant curtain raiser to the first independent organized move against the Socialist old guard. Twenty-four days later came the "Call for a National Conference of the Left wing," issued boldly over the names of the Socialist locals of Cleveland and Boston and the Left wing Section of the New York local, printed simultaneously in the Boston *Revolutionary Age* and the New York *Communist,* and a few days later, June 4, in the Ohio *Socialist.* One of the aims that Ruthenberg had discussed with John Reed and other insurgent Socialists was beginning to take shape: a Socialist Party re-organized from below. The "Call" was the rallying cry, and the *Manifesto* previously issued by the Left Wing Section of New York was the ideological basis. Delegates poured into New York from Detroit, Chicago, and a dozen other cities as well as from the initiating locals. When the Left Wing Conference met a fortnight later (June 21-24, 1919) in New York, at the Manhattan Lyceum, nine of the 94 delegates were from Ohio.[4] Outstanding at the Conference were the dynamic, fiery John Reed, Harvard-trained, of New York, and the quiet, confident C. E. Ruthenberg from the grass roots midwest town of Cleveland.

The general plan of the Conference, as Ruthenberg and a majority of the other delegates saw it, was comparatively simple: to organize themselves to take over the Socialist Party and make it a really Marxist working class political party. They were confident that the Left forces were in the majority. A Socialist Party national referendum for the election of the National Executive Committee had just been held, and enough of the returns were known—though Hillquit did not make the figures public—to show that a complete Left slate had been overwhelmingly chosen. Hillquit and his group were defeated, and Ruthenberg, Wagenknecht, Kate Richards O'Hare and John Reed got huge majorities. Ruthenberg reasoned that there was really nothing to worry about—yet, he did worry. He was beginning to understand quite objectively the unashamed dishonesty, not only of the capitalists themselves but of their Socialist apologists, and wondered what trickery Hillquit might have up his sleeve—to keep the Old Guard in office and defraud the Left of victory. When he said goodbye to Rose and Daniel on leaving for New York, he said nothing of these fears.

Here in New York, he found most of the city drab and disheartening, from the forbidding brownstone fronts of the upper west side to the squalid overcrowded lower east side. But he loved Central Park, which recalled the Rocky River Valley of Cleveland, and he reveled in the purposeful companionship of the delegates at the Conference. Here Socialist work was being done, and he was helping to guide it. There were government spies and agents swarming around, and the office of the Left Wing Section of Local New York was raided, but these things he was by now accustomed to. They were simply facets of the class struggle, and had to be systematically faced and fought.

The hectic events of the Left Wing Conference in June, and the stormy weeks from that time until the setting up of the Communist Party in September, belong more to party history than to biography. These began in New York with a split in the Left, and continued with the forming of two Communist parties—Communist and Communist Labor—in Chicago in September. Ruthenberg, while en route to Chicago, had stopped off in Detroit and elsewhere for consultations with dissident Left leaders, and made strenuous efforts to unify all factions; but no sooner did he succeed in one place than new disagreement appeared elsewhere. Unification, he discovered, required time and growth as well as idealism and logic. Foster explains in his *History of the Communist Party of the United States* that a slower, more planned and studied period of formation would have been better. And Ruthenberg himself, as Foster points out, arrived at this general conclusion in July, 1921, when he wrote in *The Communist* that most of the European communist parties were set up later than ours—*to their advantage.* In any case, Ruthenberg was chosen general secretary of the Communist Party in September, 1919, in Chicago.

While the Communist Party organizing sessions in Chicago were continuing, Ruthenberg was interviewed by a *Christian Science Monitor* reporter, who wanted to know the difference between the Communists and the Industrial Workers of the World. "The trouble with the IWW theorizing," Ruthenberg told him, according to the edition of September 16, 1919, "is that it overlooks entirely the fact that in the very process of organizing industrial unions and carrying on their strikes they run into opposition to the organized power of capitalism as embodied in the State. It is an illusion to think that the capitalists will fail to use their state power to check the development of these unions and defeat them in their strikes." Labor history illustrates how capitalists use the power of the government against strikers, Ruthenberg went on, arguing that the working class, contrary to IWW teaching, must also carry on *political* struggle. He cited the contemporary general strike in Seattle, led by the AFL, along with IWW strikes, to show how the government intervenes on the side of the capitalists. Communists are in "full accord with the industrial form of labor organization" which the IWW carries out, he said, but do not believe that the workers "can attain any high degree of industrial control without first achieving control of the power of the State."

"Criminal Syndicalism"

In the meantime, Ohio's state legislature had passed the Freeman law, forerunner of our present Smith and McCarran Acts, making it a crime to "advocate violence" as a means of securing social reform, and the authorities directed it at Ruthenberg. About the middle of July six city plainclothesmen, armed with a search warrant and assisted by members of the Loyal American League, again raided the Cleveland Socialist headquarters. Ruthenberg was at work in the office. The dicks stalked in, displayed the warrant, confiscated literature. (Only ten weeks before, members of the same gang, with no warrant at all, had raided the place.) He protested their seizure of property not named in the warrant; demanded an itemized receipt for things taken. They arrested him. Bail of $5,000 was set and furnished. The charge was violation of the new state criminal syndicalism law, the Freeman law.

The indictment, according to the *Plain Dealer,* October 29, charged Ruthenberg "with circulating copies of the *Messenger* . . . which advocates the Soviet form of government." *The Messenger,* edited by A. Phillips Randolph and Chandler Owen, was a Negro Socialist publication. "This is the fourth time Ruthenberg has been arrested within the last two months," commented the New York *Call.*[5]

While the Ohio criminal syndicalism charge against Ruthenberg was pending, a New York criminal anarchism case against him was cooked up. (The latter was given preference; the Ohio indictment was quietly dropped.) It was based on the publication of the Left Wing Manifesto by the nine-man committee elected the previous June, which included Ruthenberg and I. E. Ferguson of Chicago. The Manifesto adopted by the Left Wing Conference in June, 1919, was not greatly different from the Manifesto of the Left Wing Socialists of New York published the preceding February. The revised and completed text appeared in *The Revolutionary Age,* July 5, 1919, and it was on this act of republication that the New York case against Ruthenberg and Ferguson was based. The New York law which they had supposedly violated was the Criminal Anarchy Law of 1902, passed after the assassination of President William McKinley and aimed at terrorism. There had been no prosecutions under it for seventeen years, until the raids by the New York State Lusk Committee, forerunner of the Dies, McCarran and McCarthy Committees, suggested that the statute against terrorism might be twisted into use against Communist ideas.[6]

The trial and imprisonment of Harry Winitsky, New York organizer, merely for belonging to the Communist Party was carried out on March 15, 1920, before General Sessions Judge Bartow S. Weeks. In April, 1920, before this same judge, came the trial and conviction of James Larkin, the well-known Irish labor leader who was at that time in this country and had been involved in several labor struggles here. Benjamin Gitlow, who was then manager of a Communist publication, was also convicted at the same time. (Gitlow later became a renegade.) Then Ruthenberg and Ferguson were tried. Ruthenberg's attorney was Joseph R. Brodsky, a well-known labor and civil liberties lawyer, but in this case the 32-year-old Ferguson—a lawyer of unusual ability—did much of the legal work for both himself and Ruthenberg. Assistant District Attorney Alexander I. Rorke was the prosecutor. Ferguson filed an affidavit of prejudice against Weeks, in the light of the two preceding trials, but the latter ruled himself fit to act.[7] The indictments were brought by a special grand jury, and the trial jury was drawn from a special venire, making doubly sure of a strong class prejudice against Ruthenberg and Ferguson. Weeks—a worthy predecessor of the Judge Harold R. Medina who presided over the Communist trial of 1949—was out for a conviction. He "made a second prosecuting speech in submitting the case to the jury," the defense pointed out in a pamphlet published after the trial, and "saw to it that any possible theory of finding the defendants guilty was impressed upon the jury, regardless of the indictments."

The defense used by Ruthenberg, as in all his trials, was to present frankly and fully his reasons for thinking and acting as he did. The State was out to convict him for his views, and he made sure—as far as he could—that his views were rightly given and on the record. Government spokesmen tried to snare Ruthenberg into saying that historical explanations of events were programs for current action.[8] For example, Prosecutor Rorke said that the Basle resolution on the Socialist attitude toward war "spoke about the *desirability* of civil war in the event that the nations went to war." Ruthenberg quietly countered that the Basle resolution said something different. He explained the intent of that historic document as an expression of the workers' desire to stop the coming of imperialist war, and if it came in spite of their opposition, to use every possible means to end it.

When the time came, finally, for statements by the defendants, Ruthenberg said: "I have merely this to say for myself, that I have in the past held certain ideals for a re-organization of society on a new basis. I have upheld those ideals and gone to prison for them when they were connected with the late war. I have stood by those principles in which I firmly believe, and I will stand for those principles irrespective of the result of this particular trial. I expect in the future, as in the past, to uphold and fight for [them] until the time comes that those principles triumph, and a new society is built in place of the present social organization.

"I realized from the beginning of this trial, as I have in any other trial that I have taken part in as a defendant, that this court, and all the instruments of this court, are merely a part of that organization of force which we call the capitalist state; and I expected no other result from an organization of the capitalist class to protect the capitalist system, than the result that has been returned by this court in this particular case; and, of course, accepting this as a case of class justice, a case of the use of the organized force of the state in order to suppress the desires of those who today are suffering under the oppression of the present system, I will accept the sentence in that same spirit of defiance, realizing that I go to prison because of support of a great principle that will triumph in spite of all the courts, in spite of all the organizations of the capitalist class."

After a trial lasting nearly four weeks, Ruthenberg and Ferguson were sentenced on October 29, 1920, to from five to ten years of hard labor at Sing Sing prison.

Sing Sing Prison

"I once told you," said Ruthenberg in a letter from Sing Sing to a friend, "that the greatest deprivation of life in a prison was the absence of beauty. But here there is one form of beauty that is always ours—the Hudson river and the range of low hills on the opposite bank. Today the brisk wind has whipped up the whitecaps, and the hills are enveloped in a brilliant blue haze." The letter was dated November 10, 1920, and signed, "C. E. Ruthenberg, No. 71624."

In Sing Sing, as earlier in the Canton Workhouse, he set to work to make prison life as bearable and even as productive as possible. He read intensively. A week or so before entering prison he had read *Moon and Sixpence,* by Somerset Maugham. Now he told of reading Wells' *Research Magnificent* and Galsworthy's *The Fugitive.*

"Have you had time to finish *Jude* yet? . . . It is really worth while—one of Hardy's best," he wrote again. By December 15, he was reading Wells' *Outline of History*: "In the first three hundred pages of the book I have been sweeping through millions of years with him." He hadn't read Sinclair Lewis' *Main Street,* he wrote, in answer to a question—it had just been published that year—but he had read an earlier book, *Our Mr. Wren.* As for Gautier's *Mlle. de Maupin,* he said it was "a detestable book, beautifully written."

But he talked of other things besides books. Just before entering Sing Sing, Ruthenberg had gone to Atlanta Prison and visited Gene Debs, and in a letter he told about it. He described what a soft, affectionate human being Debs was. Debs kissed him on both cheeks, he said, and they sat down and gossiped. Ruthenberg realized later that Debs was an old, half-broken man who didn't know what the Socialist Party was really like, with its Right leadership and its loss of the Left. That—Ruthenberg felt, finally—is why Debs stuck to the old Socialist Party, the party he had founded, for which he had an unreasoned, unreasoning loyalty.

Besides reading widely, Ruthenberg signed up early in 1921 for *American History* in the Home Study correspondence department which Columbia University used to maintain. He did a good deal of the reading prescribed for the course, although the record card is marked "Closed," indicating that he did not take a final examination. He simply stopped sending in reports when his release came.

At one period during his imprisonment, as an added punitive measure, Ruthenberg was sent to Dannemora, in Clinton, New York, a prison with a severe and even cruel regime. However, he was soon transferred back to Sing Sing. At Dannemora he was not permitted to shave, but in Sing Sing he shaved every day, as if he were working in his party office back in Cleveland. In a letter dated May 23, 1921, he said: "To translate ideas into action is one of the strongest urges in me." He could not have written a more accurate description of his own character.

Seventeen-year-old Daniel Ruthenberg visited his father at Sing Sing in late 1920, in company with his mother. He went into the dull drab visiting room, where little groups of visitors sat around on iron chairs, waiting. "Then," Daniel remembers, "I saw him pop out of a door over in the corner, just like himself, except for his garb, and the prison pallor. Here was someone I knew quite well, and I knew he was all right, and here he was! With the prison guards!"

It was a short visit. They just talked a little, said hello, and asked how each other was. Ruthenberg asked what Daniel was studying. Then it was over. "When I left," Daniel says, "he came out of the prison into the yard, and waved with his arm, all the way, till I got to the top of the hill."

Ruthenberg's fellow prisoner, I. E. Ferguson, was constantly studying legal angles by which he could secure his own and Ruthenberg's release. By December, 1921, he had figured out a plan for appeal. He petitioned the New York Court of Appeals for a certificate of reasonable doubt, and eventually both secured their freedom on it.[9] After this decision, Governor Al Smith commuted the terms of Larkin and Gitlow to the time they had already served.[10]

The way Ferguson did it was as follows: He first asked the Appellate Division of the State Supreme Court for a new trial, and he and Ruthenberg both argued for it on December 6, 1921, but the Court refused. "The Appellate Division's decision ends the possibility of a new trial," the New York *Call* wrote, January 22, 1922. Then Ferguson—having no further excuse to leave prison on legal errands—got a personal friend to ask Judge Benjamin Nathan Cardozo if he would hear a petition of reasonable doubt, and received a favorable answer. Attorney Brodsky secured a writ of habeas corpus, signed by Judge Francis B. Delehanty of the First Judicial District, to get Ferguson out of Sing Sing for a day or so. Ferguson went direct to Judge Cardozo's chambers at 51 Chambers Street, New York, and argued the petition. It was granted. Brodsky then on April 22 got both Ferguson and Ruthenberg out of Sing Sing on bail for new trials (accompanied, as the *Call* notes, by two detectives of the "bomb squad"). Warden Lewis E. Lawes came personally to say good-bye to Ruthenberg.[11]

Hardly had the prisoners reached New York than they were re-arrested by orders of the convicting court, on the ground of other indictments, and were held over night in the Tombs jail, then reluctantly released. Ruthenberg went directly to a Central Executive Committee meeting, and took up his work as General Secretary of the Workers Party. On July 12, 1922, the Court of Appeals granted new trials to both men and reversed their convictions—for which they had already served a year and a half! The decision, written by Justice William S. Andrews, was concurred in by Cardozo, by Chief Justice Frank Harris Hiscock and by all the other justices except one.

Ruthenberg had a sense of real triumph as he sat in on that Workers Party central committee meeting. This was the merged communist party he had been working for, which had been formed while he was in prison. He had taken part in nearly every effort at unification from 1919 onward. But he was in Sing Sing in May, 1921, when the final unifying step was taken, and was still there at the end of the year when the Workers Party was formally set up. The new Party was the result of conferences between the existing Communist forces, now happily united, with those other Marxist groups who, during the two-year interim following the 1919 launching of the Communist movement, had deliberately separated themselves from the Socialist Party in order to help organize a more progressive and more militant political line-up.

It was a triumph in another sense, too. The United States Government had allowed the Communist movement only four months of political freedom, when the Palmer [Attorney General A. Mitchell Palmer] raids in January, 1920, tried to smash it by rounding up and jailing nearly five thousand of its leaders and workers at New Year gatherings throughout the country. Ruthenberg had insisted on a fight for full legality, and his aggressive defense in the New York trial was viewed by him as a step in that fight. In a short piece from Sing Sing which appeared August, 1921, in *The Communist,* he had written: "The Communist Party must gain prestige in the eyes of the masses.

It must win the confidence and through it the leadership of the mass of workers. Can this prestige be established and leadership won, merely through the literature of the Party—by an organization whose representatives are unknown to the workers, which they never see in action?"

The Michigan Defense Campaign

Ruthenberg's next arrest—prelude to his third prison term—came just forty days after being freed from Sing Sing. The Sing Sing sentence had been reversed on July 12, 1922. On August 21, he was seized, along with sixteen others, when the government raided a Communist meeting in Bridgman, near St. Joseph, Berrien County, Michigan. The Bridgman meeting was held on the eve of the national convention of the Workers Party, scheduled for August 28. Ruthenberg wanted to iron out differences between representatives of various factions, in order to get united support for the newly formed Workers Party, which would then at its convention plan a big anti-monopoly and anti-imperialist campaign.[12]

The gathering began on a Friday, August 18, in an old summer resort at Bridgman—a pleasant place, ideal for calm, reflective discussion—and in two days of debate disposed of most of the business at hand. Scarcely had the last vote been taken when Charles Krumbein, a close friend of Ruthenberg, discovered that a police raid was in the offing.

The arrests, as the United Press reported on August 22, were made by four deputy United States marshalls, "aided by Sheriff [George C.] Bridgman of Berrien County." The raid, the story added, was carried out "under instructions from William J. Burns, head of the Bureau of Investigation at Washington." It is important to stress that federal agents were involved, for it was not a federal but a local statute whose violation was charged: the new criminal syndicalism law passed by the Michigan legislature.[13] They were rushed to nearby St. Joseph, county seat of Berrien County, and there, chained together, with the tall, dignified Ruthenberg at their head, the seventeen Communists were paraded through the streets of the town, with the people looking on. This was a bit of crude Department of Justice drama, to persuade an unexcited public that there was danger of "force and violence" from these men.

After two days of incommunicado confinement in jail, Ruthenberg managed to send a telegram to D. J. Bentall, labor lawyer of Chicago. Bentall got Ruthenberg out on $10,000 bail on September 7, first of the defendants to receive bond. Half of his bail was raised by his wife Rose. Ruthenberg immediately took a train to New York to organize defense efforts.

Meanwhile, William Z. Foster, founder and secretary of the Trade Union Educational League, was arrested August 26 in his Chicago office, with two others, taken to St. Joseph, Michigan, and jailed with the rest of the Communist defendants. He had joined the Communist Party in 1921, during the previous summer, and was at Bridgman. He had left the meeting early, however, and was not among the seventeen arrested there, but his name—because of his importance as union and strike leader—was prominent in newspaper publicity on the case. Nineteen were now held in jail (Ruthenberg, first to be bailed out, was the twentieth), with bail set at $10,000 each; the government announced that warrants had been issued for some forty others.

While the headlines were blaring the news that Foster was jailed along with Ruthenberg, a letter was dispatched to Foster's office, signed by Roger S. Baldwin, Norman Thomas, Robert Morss Lovett, and Scott Nearing, which said: "'This is to offer you formally the services of the American Civil Liberties Union in contesting in the courts the action of the Federal and State authorities in arresting you for alleged participation in a secret Communist Convention in Michigan." When Ruthenberg reached New York, therefore, he was met halfway by friends of labor. The offer to Foster was extended to include all the Bridgman defendants.

Now began one of the biggest defense campaigns ever carried out in labor history. Baldwin insisted that the noted attorney and liberal, Frank P. Walsh, be engaged as chief counsel, and Ruthenberg agreed. A legal staff was set up under Walsh which included Walter Nelles, Detroit labor lawyer, and Humphrey S. Gray, local attorney of Benton Harbor, Michigan.

Two defense committees were organized. One was the "Labor

Defense Council," with headquarters in Chicago, which included—among others—Roger N. Baldwin of the American Civil Liberties Union; Elizabeth Gurley Flynn of the Workers Defense Union; Max S. Hayes, old-time friend of Ruthenberg and editor of the Cleveland *Citizen;* Eugene V. Debs, now out of the Atlanta federal penitentiary; John G. Brown, national secretary of the Farmer-Labor Party; and Robert M. Buck, editor of *New Majority,* official organ of the Chicago Federation of Labor and also of the Farmer-Labor Party. The other group was the "Committee of the Defendants," headed by Ruthenberg and Foster.

The high cost of bail and legal defense made money-raising one of the big problems. Foster's bail was quickly raised by the trade unions, but it was December 22, before all the remaining eighteen could be bailed out. The last four were released for $5,000 each after persistent pleas by defense counsel and protests by liberals and workers. Elizabeth Gurley Flynn was sent first on a fund-raising tour; then Foster and Ruthenberg, routed together on a joint tour of the eastern states. The goal was to raise $100,000.

On the insistence of Ruthenberg, defense policy was carefully formulated. Baldwin and he were appointed a sub-committee to draw up an agreement, and among the motions they made, adopted by the Labor Defense Council, was the following: "In case of a difference of opinion arising between Labor Defense Committee and Committee of the Defendants, that a decision be contingent upon a majority vote of both national committee and committee representing defendants." They set forth two parallel purposes: "For the defense of the Michigan Criminal Syndicalist defendants prosecuted at the instance of the Federal Secret Service in its drive against organized labor; to carry on in connection with the legal defense, a campaign against all infringements upon the rights of free speech, free press and freedom of assemblage and all measures restricting the rights of the workers."

The legal defense in the courts was to rest on constitutional guarantees of free speech and organization. A meeting was held at Bridgman and matters were discussed: the contention would be that they had a right to so meet and discuss. There were other matters of defense policy that had to be agreed on, as shown by a memo of Baldwin's of September 18: "I shall, therefore, take up all the details with Ruthenberg here when he comes, and endeavor to get an agreement on the main lines of the campaign."[14] One such "detail" was a dictum by Baldwin that no defendant should take the stand, and that the defense would consist chiefly of a cross-examination of the government witnesses. Such a negative defense plan did not satisfy Ruthenberg, and he and Foster both took the stand in their own defense. As Ruthenberg's friend Krumbein explained years later, speaking of Ruthenberg's bold and militant attitude in the courtroom, "The Bridgman defense was—objectively—a campaign for full legalization of the Party." Headquarters of the defense was in Chicago, in the office of the Trade Union Educational League of which Foster was secretary. The leaders of the Chicago Federation of Labor, who all knew Foster personally, supported the defense. *New Majority,* organ of the Chicago Federation, helped inform the American labor movement about the issues in the trial.

The background of the government's raid on Bridgman was one of militant industrial unrest. Half a million coal miners were on strike, as well as 400,000 railroad shopmen and 200,000 textile workers. As labor lawyer Walter Nelles pointed out, the employers especially wanted to "get" Foster, AFL organizer, who had led the Steel Strike in 1919 and whose prestige and influence were high. The employers were alarmed even more at the newly organized amalgamation movement led by the Trade Union Educational League which Foster headed, a movement which for several months before the trial had been making tremendous headway (especially among railroad workers and in the building trades) with its program of merging the craft unions into industrial unions. This is why Foster was first of the Communists to be brought to trial. A *New Majority* editorial said it was clear "that the cause of the victims of the Daugherty [Attorney General Harry M. Daugherty] raids is the concern of the labor movement and that an attack on 'reds' is an overt attack on unionism." The Michigan State Federation of Labor called on Governor Alex J. Groesbeck of Michigan to quash the indictments against the men arrested in the "red raids."

Ruthenberg for his part vigorously defended the political activities of the Communists. In a speech before the trials, he ridiculed the propaganda about the "secret underground reds." The published photographs of the arrested men, he pointed out, showed them "surrounded by typewriters, mimeographs, and printed matter . . . not cannons or guns or bombs." They were arrested, he said, not because of any threat of violence but "because they were trying to spread their ideas through use of typewriters and mimeographs." "The Communist Party of America," he went on, "was organized in 1919 at a convention held in the city of Chicago. There was nothing secret about this convention. There was nothing underground about the organization it created." The Communists, he explained, as citizens of the United States exercising their legal political rights, took it for granted that the constitutional guarantees of free speech were real, and that they applied to them as well as to others. Then, he said, came the Palmer raids, the deportations, the prison sentences. "That was the answer which the Communists received to their acting on the assumption that even Communists had the right of free speech, free press and freedom of assemblage in the United States."[15]

In the March, 1923, *Liberator,* in an article written on the eve of the trial and published while the trial was on, Ruthenberg calmly discussed the question of "violence" which loomed so large in newspaper propaganda against himself and Foster. It was the Burns and other detective agencies, and the government police, that supply the violence in labor "trouble," he pointed out. "No Communist advocates the use of violence in the class struggle in the United States today," he wrote. "Communists have better sense." While he was thus skirmishing on the issue of the case, striving for public understanding and getting ready to wage the court battle, Ruthenberg kept his eyes on the larger issue of Communist progress. In another *Liberator* article shortly before the trial opened, he had a report on the second convention of the Workers Party held in New York beginning December 24, just four months after it had been originally scheduled and only two days after the last Bridgman defendant had been bailed out. He said the concept of workers' rule, which had first been stated in an American political program in September, 1919, was now in the program of the Workers Party. The convention, he went on, recognized that American workers would not "over night become converted to Communism," and that what was now needed was a "step by step" growth into Marxist methods of thinking and action.[16]

While separate trials were agreed to for each of the twenty defendants, only two were actually brought to trial: Foster and Ruthenberg. Foster's trial came first, on March 12, 1923. Four indictments had been brought against the twenty under the Michigan criminal syndicalism act, and not one of them charged any overt act of sabotage or violence. The first three contained charges of *advocating* or *teaching* violent overthrow of the government, and these three were quashed by Judge Charles W. White at the start of the trial, on motion of Attorney Walsh. The fourth indictment was based on a section of the statute which denounced as guilty anyone who "becomes a member of or voluntarily *assembles with* [Emphasis added] any society, group or assemblage of persons formed to teach or advocate" violence to bring about reform. The words "assemble with" became famous in this case. "Assembling with" became a new crime in labor history, a prototype of the "guilt by association" of the later Smith Act trials. As *New Majority* reported in a headline on March 24, "Assembling With Is Foster's Crime."

One of the first stories on the Foster trial in the weekly *Worker*, established by the Workers Party immediately after the Party was formed, was by Ruthenberg himself, dealing with the drawing of the jury and date-lined "Courthouse, St. Joseph, Mich." The dingy but silghtly pompous courtroom, now all of a sudden bristling with unaccustomed importance as the proceedings got under way, was filled with townspeople. Ruthenberg sat among them, jotting down notes for the Communist newspaper, and studied the actions and attitudes of the two chief opposition lawyers, O. L. Smith, Michigan state attorney, and

Charles W. Gore, prosecuting attorney of Berrien County.

Defense attorney Gray, according to Ruthenberg's account, was trying to find out how much the newspaper "force and violence" propaganda had prejudiced prospective jurors. Suppose, he explained, in questioning them, the defendant is convinced that the capitalists will not give up their privileges without violence, regardless of the wishes of the majority of the people. The defendant does not believe in force or violence now, but he thinks that in the end, when the people have decided they want socialism, force will be needed to put down the capitalists who violently oppose socialism. Would the juror, then, be prejudiced against him? The juror, hesitating, thought he might be. "Then," Gray said, "you believe that the Declaration of Independence should be suppressed because it advocated the fundamental right of the people to revolution, if necessary by force?" Prosecutor Smith jumped to his feet, objecting angrily to such an interpretation of the Declaration of Independence. Gray offered to read a letter written by Thomas Jefferson, to clarify the document's meaning, and again Smith shouted, "We object to getting the influence of Thomas Jefferson on the minds of this jury!"

Thus the trial, following Ruthenberg's plan, assumed an educational pattern, a persistent exposition of American democratic principles, of American libertarian traditions. Robert Minor, the great artist and journalist, who also sat in the courtroom looking on, stressed this instructional aspect of the court defense in another article in the *Worker,* as the questioning of the jurors continued. The crowd, he wrote, listened "with peculiar wondering attentiveness" to these new ideas that were nonetheless strangely reasonable. "Do you know," the defense attorney went on, "that *proletariat* means people who work? If evidence shows Foster to have been leader and spokesman of 380,000 steel workers during the great steel strike of 1919, would that prejudice you against him? If evidence shows that provocateurs deliberately provoked violation of law in order to convict another for it, would you give credence to that man's word?"

Frequently, in these opening days, Robert Minor reported, defense attorney Walsh made reference to the First, Second and

Third Internationals, along with reference to international associations of business men and chambers of commerce. Walsh asked prospective jurors "whether they believe workers have the same right to organize international associations as capitalists have." The jury was selected at last, and included on it nine farmers, one non-union railway worker, one non-union grocery clerk, and one woman, a housewife.

The defense offered only two witnesses, Ruthenberg, as an expert on communism, to counter the Department of Justice "experts," and Foster himself, the defendant. As a witness, Ruthenberg was on the stand for more than four days in all—over a day for direct testimony and three full days for cross-examination. With the same quiet confidence as in the New York trial, and with greater skill, he strove for the fullest explanation of Marxist-Leninist teachings possible under courtroom conditions. Attorney Walsh battled prosecution objections for permission for Ruthenberg to make a complete statement of Communist principles. "It is Communist principles which are on trial here in the person of William Z. Foster," Walsh declared. And a good deal of Communist theory *was* presented, despite obstacles.

Prosecutor Gore tried at first, to his cost, to bait Ruthenberg. "You believe the government of the United States is a capitalist government, do you not?" he asked, and Ruthenberg said "Yes." Then: "You believe the government of the State of Michigan is a capitalist government? You believe this court is a capitalist court?" Ruthenberg said "Yes." But when he said, "You believe this jury is a capitalist jury?" Ruthenberg said, "The jury? No, that's a different matter." But Gore would not let Ruthenberg explain why the jury was a different matter. A few minutes later, however, Walsh brought it out in re direct examination. Ruthenberg showed that it was possible for a jury, even in a capitalist court, to return verdicts in favor of workers instead of capitalists, if the jury contained workers or farmers not dominated by capitalist ideas. The prosecutor fought hard to prevent the question being answered, then tried to have the answer stricken from the record.

Around the first of April the worried prosecution asked for

a recess to present a motion that Ruthenberg's testimony "and further testimony that he might give" be stricken from the record, but it was too late. Judge White ruled that the testimony was not objected to when Ruthenberg took the stand, and that objection could not be made now after he had testified for many hours, in both direct and cross-examination. Ruthenberg resumed the stand for further devastating but truthful explanations of Communist principles. "Ruthenberg's testimony produced a most favorable effect upon the jury and public sentiment," Foster wrote in the *Labor Herald,* May, 1923. "The prosecution was plainly appalled by it." Their "futile attempt to get rid of him and to strike out his testimony" was a "humiliating defeat" for them, he stressed.

Foster himself testified next, more briefly. Department of Justice versions of his speech to the Bridgman meeting were so garbled that he insisted on reproducing it in court, so that an accurate account would be in the record. The jury was out 31 hours and took 36 ballots. On every ballot the result was six for conviction and six for acquittal, with the lone housewife, Mrs. Minerva Olson, the grocer clerk, Russell Durm, and four farmers voting steadily from the first for a verdict of innocent. Judge White discharged the jury; while technically Foster might be tried again, the result was in effect a vindication.

All this time, during the Foster trial and the Ruthenberg trial which followed, the Committee of the Defendants labored to inform the public on the main issue of the case, the question (as Ruthenberg said again and again) whether constitutional rights apply to *everybody*—whether, in fact, they are ours when we need them! Members of the Workers Party were asked to contribute a day's pay. Tom Mooney from his cell in San Quentin called for help for the Michigan defendants. From faraway Tokyo the Japanese Communist Party sent a message of sympathy. Art Young drew a cartoon for the *Worker* entitled "The Department of Justice Training School," showing how sleuths can learn to use "manufactured evidence" or a "bought witness," or how to wear a disguise and peer into workers' homes on hands and knees.

Ruthenberg's trial was set for April 16. The prosecution

proceeded with extreme caution and extreme vindictiveness in this next trial. Ruthenbrg, who had been on the witness stand for four days in the Foster trial, was allowed only an hour to testify in his own. Only property holders this time were allowed on the jury: no wage workers, and no women at all. Biased and fraudulent tactics (now common in Smith Act trials) were used by the government to prevent Ruthenberg from explaining communism to this second jury, and the character of the proceedings was changed from a trial to a witchhunt, as *Worker* correspondent Clarissa S. Ware explained in a summary article. There was a steady, persistent appeal to the jurors' prejudices, minute by minute, hour by hour; and a successful effort to work on Judge White, getting him to modify the old-fashioned, strictly impartial rulings he had been making in the Foster case.

The prosecution quoted from Marxist literature passages giving "a Communist viewpoint on what science has to say about religion," and kept reading such passages until the worried judge warned against going too far afield. Similarly, with great patriotic fervor about "our boys fighting in Europe," the prosecution told the jury that Ruthenberg had opposed the war and been convicted in court of so doing. The defense objected over and over, but in vain. To all of these irrelevances was added an intentional confusing of the "force and violence" charge by tearing from their context all references to force—regardless of their historic perspective, regardless of whether or not there was any hint of immediate advocacy—and reading these, by the hour, to the perplexed jury. Efforts by the defense to get permission for Ruthenberg to explain the language and the background of these passages were blocked.

In the wind-up of the case Judge White came to the assistance of the prosecution in his charge to the jury. In the Foster case, he had told the jury that Communists had the right to advocate communism and "the Soviet form of government" anywhere in the United States. In the Ruthenberg case, as the *Worker* article reported, he gave new instructions: "It is the contention of the prosecution that the advocacy of the Soviets *includes the advocacy of force* because the Soviets, the prosecutors claimed, could not be established without the use of force."

Following this hypothesis, Judge White told the jury that if the Communist Party advocated the Soviet form of government, they must bring in a verdict of guilty. Even so, two jurymen voted for acquittal on the first two ballots. On the third ballot, rendered on May 2, 1923, the verdict was guilty. Because an immediate appeal was made to the Michigan Supreme Court, Judge White deferred sentencing Ruthenberg until the higher court had made its ruling.

The sequel to this bit of history came a year and a half later, December 9, 1924, when the Michigan Supreme Court not only upheld Ruthenberg's conviction but issued a mandate to Judge White to pronounce sentence. The Michigan high court would not withdraw the mandate when Ruthenberg's attorneys announced appeal to the United State Supreme Court, and refused to grant bail. Ruthenberg was sentenced to from three to ten years and taken to Jackson state prison, which he entered January 5, 1925.

In his statement after sentencing, he said simply that he had advocated the principles of communism, and had openly expressed his support of them from the witness stand. "I deny that there is anything 'criminal' in these principles," he said. He posed the question, what *are* the Workers Party ideas for which "the state of Michigan, acting as the agent of the capitalist class, desires to imprison me?" He continued: "I have argued that the working masses must organize their power under the leadership of the Communists to establish a workers' and farmers' government which will rule in *their* interests in place of that of the exploiters. I have urged that only such a government could reorganize our social structure to abolish exploitation and oppression and to make industry serve the happiness and well-being of those who produce the wealth of the country." He reminded the court that capitalism had already taken the world into one World War, and "if what is good in our civilization is to be saved, if mankind is to go forward to a saner and finer life," it could only happen if the workers struggled on until they established a workers' and farmers' government and began "the rebuilding of our social order and the creation of a communist society." That is the thinking of the party, he finished, "with which I am charged with assembly and of which I am proud to be a member."

Ruthenberg served twenty days before his attorneys secured a writ of supersedeas from Supreme Court Justice Louis Brandeis and $7,500 bail. (Justice James C. McReynolds had refused to grant the writ.) Ruthenberg was out of prison in time to address a Lenin memorial meeting in New York. Lenin had died a year earlier—January 21, 1924.

In his first published statement after leaving Jackson prison, Ruthenberg called for a fight against the threat of sending thirty or forty other defendants to prison. So far, he said, drily, victory lay with the workers, for "The best that the capitalist class has been able to do two years and five months after the raid on the Communist convention at Bridgman is to put me in prison for three weeks."

Actually, although Robert Minor's trial was set for February, it was never held. The Department of Justice was having its own troubles. The Department's head, Attorney General Harry M. Daugherty, Republican, had been removed from office because of involvement in the Teapot Dome oil scandal, and William J. Burns, whose agents made the raid at Bridgman, had lost his Secret Service job. There were no more Bridgman trials, and Ruthenberg, out of prison, threw himself full time into the activities of the Workers Party, which by now officially called itself the Workers (Communist) Party.

10

HERALD OF THE UNITED FRONT

RUTHENBERG felt a great deal of optimism after the Bridgman trial. He had a satisfying confidence that the way was now cleared for working class progress. True, he had been found "guilty," appeals to higher courts would have to follow, and there was the threat of another prison term. But the Workers Party, with an office in Chicago, was forged, unity was achieved, legality was conquered. He was free, now, to drive ahead and win the people for socialism. Himself a man of unusual probity and unusual intelligence, he felt utmost faith in appealing to people's minds and hearts. He never ceased to believe that if Communists simply relied on the mental clarity and genuine honesty of the workers, they would win these workers' full support.

He was now forty-one years old, and no one dreamed that he had only three more years to go. He was in vigorous health, and had tremendous energy and endurance. He would take part in grueling all-night sessions on committees and at conventions, and appear fresh and ready for work in the morning. He had no excess weight, was in fact as slender now in early 1923 as in 1912 at Indianapolis, in 1917 at St. Louis, in 1919 at the Left Wing Convention in New York. He had the same deliberate, quietly confident manner; now he was getting bald, but his skin was clear and a little ruddy, and his eyes were blue and direct. He was a rock-like man, says Foster—who knew him from 1921 on: he could neither be pushed around nor maneuvered about. In personal conference he was soft-spoken, rather reticent, and always courteous; on the public platform, when he felt that he spoke not for himself but for the working class, he was aggressive, eloquent, powerful. His vision was never restricted to the day or the place or the current happening; he kept in mind the needs of the party and the state of the nation, while dealing with the matter of the moment. A court trial, no matter how crucial, was incidental to the party's larger struggle. Going to jail or prison was a subordinate part of the class conflict. But he never neglected these subordinate tasks. He fought the little fights as well as the big ones.

Late in May, 1923, right after the Michigan trials, an ellegedly Communist "manifesto"—a forgery apparently drawn up by some of Burns' Secret Service operatives, predecessors of our present FBI—was circulated here and there in a few localities, with of course provocative intent. Ruthenberg smilingly took time to discuss it in the *Worker*. He ridiculed it for spelling *Communist* with one *m*, for telling the workers to act through "Force of Arms," and for its idiotic shriek, "Prepare! Prepare! Prepare!" No Communist could ever write such a leaflet, he pointed out, and no intelligent worker would ever give it a second look. What the Communists really wanted, he explained in a new pamphlet: *Why Every Worker Should Be a Communist and Join the Workers Party*, with drawings by Robert Minor and Fred Ellis. Ruthenberg wrote in simple language that Communists had both a long-view plan, that is, socialism, and a short-view plan, that is, the things that workers were talking about now and wanted right away, such as decent wages, a shorter workday, and job security. He called particularly, as part of a short-view plan, for a labor party, the amalgamation of craft into industrial unions, the organization of the unorganized, and "complete social equality for the Negro."

But a prerequisite for a labor party, he believed, was a strong Workers Party, and a prerequisite for *that* was a daily press, and this was the next task he set himself. The weekly *Worker* had been set up while he was in Sing Sing, when the Workers Party was formed. It was named after a weekly which had been published some years earlier by the Socialist Party of New York, before the starting of the New York *Call* in 1909. The new *Worker* was an amalgamation of several Left papers, notably the *Workers Council*, a temporary publication by the newest Left wing in the Socialist Party, which had seceded in order to help form the Workers Party; and the *Toiler*, a Communist organ, which in its turn was the successor of the Ohio *Socialist* and Ruthenberg's *Socialist News.*

In the paper's first issue, published February 2, 1922, had appeared the words, "This, the first issue of the *Worker*, is the advance agent of the *Daily Worker.*" Now, more than a year later, Ruthenberg wanted that announcement to be carried into action, and for that purpose undertook an unremitting publicity campaign. First came a drive to raise $100,000 to start it off. Ruthenberg wrote ironically in the *Worker* that in America there were already several excellent working class dailies—*in foreign languages.*[1] After many weeks, the *Daily Worker* was definitely launched in Chicago, January 15, 1924, with J. Louis Engdahl, formerly editor of the Chicago *Socialist,* as first editor, and a small staff of editorial workers. It was an epochal event. But for Ruthenberg, with his purposive energy and devoted hopes, it was less an achievement than a starting point, as indeed it was.

There was ferment among the Negro people, and the new daily paper reported happenings of interest to them, hitherto to be found only in the Negro press. Late in 1924 the paper carried a copy of a friendly greeting sent by Ruthenberg and Foster, as secretary and chairman, respectively, of the Workers Party, to the Universal Negro Improvement Association, led by Marcus Garvey, one of the popular protest movements among the Negro people at that time, which centered, however, upon a back-to-Africa program. The greeting included a pointed suggestion: "The rights of the Negro in Africa are not free for the taking. They have to be fought for, no less than the rights of the Negro in America."

The Farmer-Labor Party

The progressive working class program of the time was to merge the craft unions into effective industrial organizations and to get a third party that would deserve and win the votes of millions of workers and farmers. Ruthenberg was thinking of a labor party such as existed in England, in which Communist trade unionists participated. The Communists in the United States—that is, the Workers Party—would be in it and support it, and, he hoped, might leaven it and influence its policies. The Communists wished to maintain the separate identity of the Workers Party *within* the labor party, because they had an ultimate goal: socialism. But they wanted at the same time to advance the workers' immediate interests, by participating in the day-to-day struggle along with the larger group which had as yet no "ultimate" goal of social change.

The vast majority in this larger group would not, he thought, object to the Communists' short-range program. There could be no disagreement *among workers* on the immediate objectives: higher wages, shorter hours, better working conditions, unemployment benefits, equal rights for oppressed groups (Negroes and foreign-born), greater workers' share in running the government. The bigger and more inclusive the workers' unity, the surer and quicker their achievement of these common aims. But there were obstacles to such a plan. Some of them Ruthenberg knew and expected, and others he did not expect, or underestimated, or knew nothing of until they showed themselves. Foster, more than thirty years later, in *Political Affairs*, December, 1955, commented on the "failure [of the American working class] to produce a broad mass Labor-Farmer Party."

The first opportunity for a start at anything along this line had come just before the Michigan trials, at a meeting of the Conference for Progressive Political Action, held in Cleveland, December 11-12, 1922. Ruthenberg and Foster, out on bail and busy with defense work, took time to attend it as delegates of the Workers Party. There was an off-chance that the Conference's small group of militant trade union representatives would get the city central labor bodies of Chicago and Detroit moving in the direction of independent political action. The latter groups apparently favored a labor party if it were not too much trouble. But there was another group headed by the railroad union leaders and the chiefs of the still-existing Socialist Party, and *they* had no intention of forming a labor party.

The story of the Conference was written up by Ruthenberg, with rather bitter humor, in the *Liberator*.[2] Morris Hillquit, it appears, was there in person, and through tricks of parliamentary law, blocked the seating of not only Foster and Ruthenberg but the delegates of several militant trade unions too. The way he did it was gall and wormwood to Ruthenberg, who was himself a skilled parliamentarian. It seems that the credentials committee, loaded with safe bureaucrats, did two things: first, they recommended that the contested union delegates be not seated, and second, they made no mention whatever of Workers Party delegates. But a credentials committee minority recommended that the union delegates be seated, and the Conference overwhelmingly adopted the minority report. This meant, or should have meant, that these trade union delegates were admitted. But no. "Mr. Hillquit"—Ruthenberg's report said—"rose to make a point of order," and said that the vote just taken simply meant that the Conference "did not concur" in the credentials committee majority report, and moved that the matter go back to the credentials committee. The chairman so ruled—"And the center group let them get away with it!" —Ruthenberg wrote.

That wasn't all. Ruthenberg addressed the chair and demanded a report on the Workers Party credentials—that is, his own and Foster's—which had not been mentioned, and the committee chairman replied blandly that no such credentials had been received! (They were found later, but some self-appointed overseer had simply laid them aside.) Thus the Conference was able to proceed smoothly with a do-nothing program, only a Right and Center taking part. There were no vigorous proponents of a labor party, and none was formed. The stage was set for endorsement, two years later, of old-party candidates, perhaps with a reform label. This had been the first post-war opening for independent political action by labor in the United States, and labor had lost it. Ruthenberg and Foster went back to the Michigan courtroom to fight through their battle there. But a second chance for a labor party came after the trial, on July 2, 1923, in Ashland Auditorium, Chicago.

The story in brief was as follows: The midwest Farmer-Labor Party, a sectional political group combining Minesota and Dakota farmers and Chicago trade unionists, invited labor and progressive bodies all over the country to attend its convention for the purpose of forming a nation-wide organization, and one of the invitations came to the Workers Party. It was signed by John G. Brown, national secretary of the Farmer-Labor Party—the same John G. Brown who, along with Roger Baldwin and Eugene Debs, had been on the Labor Defense Council which fought for Foster and Ruthenberg in the trials just past. The planned over-all farmer-labor party, said Brown, "should not interfere with the autonomy of any of the affiliated bodies," but should be "a federation of federations." The auspices were friendly, and the conditions were propitious. The Workers Party sent delegates, with Ruthenberg as chief spokesman.

At the opening session, John Fitzpatrick, President of the Chicago Federation of Labor, keynoted the meeting for unity. "How foolish and ridiculous it is for the workers to be divided," he said, "when the bosses of Big Business are united everywhere. . . . We are going to come out of this conference with some sort of an arrangement, some kind of solution, some sort of a working agreement that will centralize our efforts, and cause all of our difficulties to vanish."

But already pressures were on him and on Brown to edge away from the Communists. The Socialist group, though invited, sent no representatives. And now the sponsoring Farmer-Labor Party proposed setting apart their own "duly authorized" delegates from the others, which aroused resentment. The Farmer-Labor chairman dead-locked every motion by holding tenaciously to the point of order that this was the narrow F-LP convention (contrary to the wording of the invitations that had been sent to the other groups), and the meeting was getting nowhere until Ruthenberg moved an adjournment to the next morning when the full "Farmer-Labor Conference" would be formally called together.

Came the morning, and Joseph Manley, delegate of the Bridge and Structural Iron Workers, moved that the meeting declare itself in favor of forming a Federated Farmer-Labor Party and set up immediately an organizing committee for the purpose. The motion—after some talk of amendments—was ruled out of order. Here Ruthenberg got the floor. "We came here to do what the *Call* [issued by the Farmer-Labor Party of the midwest] asked us to come here and do," he said. Reviewing the sentiment all over the country for a labor party, he declared that the workers and farmers "are waiting for some organization around which they can rally and fight the exploiters of this country." Since the purpose of the meeting was to form a labor party, and since labor in farm and factory throughout the land was calling for it, the first step was to do what Manley's motion asked, and he re-introduced it, whereupon it was immediately adopted by a huge majority. This proposal—known from then on as the "Ruthenberg-Manley motion"—became the bone of contention over which the narrow Farmer-Labor delegates, who were too few to split the convention by withdrawing, tried to wreck the meeting.

Fitzpatrick and Brown became bitter, and made veiled charges against an alleged "group" trying to dominate the proceedings. Rank and file delegates charged that these leaders had obtained a bigger response to their Call for a Conference than they expected, and were scared by success. It was a critical moment.

Ruthenberg took the floor again, greeted with applause, and tried to soften the animosity and the bitterness. He pointed out that the Farmer-Labor Party had sent out its own *Call,* that its own credentials committee had organized the Conference and approved the delegates, that the Committee of Twenty-Nine which brought in the suggested Program and Constitution had voted 26 to 3 for it, and that with this broad basis neither the new party nor its program could be labeled Communist. The Workers Party, he said, only wanted a broad labor party to exist, they didn't want to run it. Its delegates agreed that the Farmer-Labor Party should be "the foremost group in the new Party," he said, "but we draw the line at failure to secure united action in this gathering. We cannot concede that the unifying organization should not be formed here."

So the Federated Farmer-Labor Party was formed, then and there, but the regional Farmer-Labor Party withdrew. The new Labor Party "failed to win the masses," as Foster says in the *History,*[3] and, without adherents, it simply faded from the paper it was written on.

A third try took place in St. Paul, Minnesota, the following year, June 17, 1924. An even broader representation this time brought together spokesmen of the various state Farmer-Labor parties and various semi-political farmer and trade union groups, along with the Workers Party. Ruthenberg endeavored to steer the Conference in the direction of a party intentionally dominated by workers and farmers, consciously oriented toward struggle against the big employers and bankers. Jay Brown and his colleagues were present, and this time they indulged in open—not covert—red-baiting. But a clear majority maintained a tolerant unity. They calmly formed the National Farmer-Labor Party, and nominated candidates for president and vice-president for the 1924 election campaign.

Seventeen days later, however—on July 4th—another meeting of the Conference for Progressive Political Action was held in Cleveland at which Senator Robert M. La Follette (who had already announced his candidacy) was nominated for president, on La Follette's own published platform. Under the magic of La Follette's name the expected constituencies of the National Farmer-Labor Party melted away, and its national board withdrew its candidates from the campaign. When this happened, the Workers Party announced that it would have its own national ticket, headed by William Z. Foster for president.

Ruthenberg was able on July 9 to offer a cool, well-reasoned appraisal of the La Follette nominating convention which had wrecked the National Farmer-Labor Party. It was "not to be ignored or lightly laid aside," he wrote. Labor was represented there, he said, largely by the leaders of the railroad unions, among whom there was sentiment for nationalizing the railroads, but the dominant leadership was in the hands of the middle class. La Follette's appeal was to "little business as well as to the industrial workers and farmers." La Follette, he said, wanted chiefly a curbing of "private monopoly" through the Sherman anti-trust act.

Ruthenberg and Foster attended the convention which nominated La Follette, right in Ruthenberg's home town, and saw it all at first hand, as the former reported in the *Daily Worker* of July 7. They got admission cards, he said, "with our names duly written thereon," and, walking toward the balcony, asked directions of the sergeant-at-arms. "He glanced at us and a look of horror appeared on his face. Throwing up his arms to make impossible our passing him, he shouted to his assistants: 'Call the police!'

"We inquired what it was all about, and he informed us that he and all other sergeants-at-arms had been given instructions to keep us out of the hall. We mildly asked why all the excitement, and after some urging, got the news that we were expected to try to capture the convention and the leaders had determined that we should not."

The two Communists assured the man they had no interest in capturing the convention. The distressed fellow, Ruthenberg wrote, "softened a bit and informed Foster, evidently to clear himself, 'I voted for Ruthenberg for mayor and went to school with him. I wouldn't do this, but I've got to carry out instructions.' "

Finally the chief guard told him, "Oh, let them in," and the two took their seats.

In the process of self-criticism and evaluation of the work that followed the labor party efforts, debate became cleavage, and contrary views grew into factions within the Workers Party. Out of an honest difference of opinion over the tactics and timing of the Labor party undertaking developed a serious inner party controversy which was not finally resolved until more than a year after Ruthenberg's death. The matter is set forth in Foster's *History*,[4] and there is no point in going into it here. Ruthenberg's aim from 1919 on had been, in Elizabeth Gurley Flynn's words, "to consolidate the different groups and get them to work together," and his name attached to a faction is therefore a seeming anomaly. His unwilling involvement was, historically, merely an incident in this difficult period of party history.

Last Days

Though the inner-party controversy smoldered, Ruthenberg did not permit his main energies to be smothered under it

Throughout 1926 he re-doubled his efforts to build the Workers Party and to reach new sections of workers and of the people. In the spring he wrote a short introduction for a souvenir edition of pictures of the Paris Commune. "History has raised an imperishable monument to the Commune," he said. "In the Soviet Union the proletariat . . . has erected a Commune, not of one town . . . but of . . . over one-sixth of the globe." And he added: "The American workers also have their heroic traditions of struggle. We have much to learn from the experiences of the Communards—we who face the most powerful and most ruthless class enemy the world has ever known, the American bourgeoisie."

Later he began a series in the *Daily Worker* on "Many Opportunities for Building the Revolutionary Movement."[5] He criticized those who were pessimistic about the possibilities of drawing the American workers into a militant class struggle and really building a Communist movement here. With 25,-000,000 unorganized wage-earners in the country, he argued, there was but one thing to do: go to them, teach them, organize them.

As time rounded the corner of 1926 and raced on into 1927, no one thought that in sixty days Ruthenberg would be dead.

With his usual vigor and enthusiasm he was making plans for the new year, surveying the capitalist economy, and planning to write a history of the party. In the first days of January he gave a series of three lectures in Chicago on the "History of the Communist Movement in the United States."

Later in the month, President Coolidge sent a jingoistic message about the situation in Nicaragua, where resentment at dollar imperialism was flaring into revolt. He had stationed United States warships off the Nicaraguan coast. Ruthenberg responded by sending a signed statement, on behalf of the Workers (Communist) Party, to the American Federation of Labor, the Socialist Party, the Industrial Workers of the World, and to the independent unions and farmers' organizations urging them to fight against the danger of a new war. "Labor," he urged, "must demand hands off Nicaragua, Mexico, and China! [American gunboats were at that time in Chinese waters, too.]

No sacrifice of American lives for Wall Street investment!"

In the *Daily Worker* he analyzed "Coolidge's war policy for Wall Street imperialism," noting that in his message the President, in excusing his intervention in Nicaragua, had shamelessly spoken of "large investments" in lumbering, mining, coffee growing, banana culture, shipping and other business in that small country. When Secretary of State Frank B. Kellogg announced, a day or so later, that "We are fighting 'Red' plots" in Nicaragua, Ruthenberg replied that the use of the " 'Red' scare" was an "unfailing method" of uniting the big and little capitalists for some imperialist chicanery.

Before the month was out, Ruthenberg spoke at a Lenin memorial meeting, reminding his audience that Lenin had explained the rise of modern imperialism, and pointing out that the United States was even then robbing and oppressing our sister republics to the south.

At the beginning of February he analyzed capitalist reports on the past year's profits and the coming year's expectations. He headed his article, "First Signs of a Downward Trend in Industry," and pointed to some of the figures released by the Department of Labor. These, he said, threw "a wet blanket" on the "prosperity shouters." He commented that the figures indicated "a general recession in production with an increase in unemployment," although it did not appear that there would be a crisis "for some months yet." Then he added: "The tendency of industry, however, is downward. How deep-going the depression will be is not yet apparent, but that it is in the offing is indicated by all the factors governing industry."[6] The economic crisis actually matured two years later, in the great collapse of 1929.

It is clear that Ruthenberg had not the slightest notion of a "Golden Age of Capitalism," the "exceptionalist" doctrine which Jay Lovestone was already formulating and which he openly advocated after Ruthenberg's death. Lovestone was expelled for disruptive factionalism in 1929—with the coming of the crisis.

For eight years Ruthenberg had tirelessly been trying to unify into one party all organizations with a Communist viewpoint, and now he addressed himself to the last remaining group on the outside, the Proletarian Party—the same "Michigan group," interestingly enough, which, headed by John Keracher, Detroit Socialist, had led the secession from the Left Wing Conference back in June, 1919, and had then joined in issuing the call to organize the Communist Party in September, 1919. They had withdrawn later and, while Ruthenberg was at Sing Sing, had formed their own small party. In the *Daily Worker* of February 28—in a piece written four days before his death—he appealed to "our Proletarian Party friends" to join forces with the Workers Party, "the only living force in the American labor movement today" that was trying to organize and lead the workers against the capitalists. In a conciliatory manner he expressed awareness of the fact that the Proletarian Party devoted most of its energies to the classroom study of Marx and Engels, and praised this work. But he added that "the knowledge gained in study-classes must be carried into the actual class struggle," and how was the Proletarian Party doing anything of this kind? "Every conscious and understanding Communist," he wrote, "is needed, and should give his services where they can achieve the greatest results." (The Proletarian Party declined the invitation. It still exists in Chicago and other cities, in the form of Marxist study groups.)

In late February, as Alexander Trachtenberg remembers, Ruthenberg came to New York to meet with New York members of the Central Executive Committee. In his hotel room, where they conferred, Ruthenberg suddenly doubled up in pain.

"Oh, I've got that trouble again," he apologized. It was a sharp pain in the appendix region, which had been bothering him, off and on, for a week or more.

"Well," the others said, with concern, "let's get you a doctor. Or take you to a hospital."

He shook his head. "No," he said, his time-table of work always in mind, "there isn't time. I've got to get to that meeting in Chicago."

Actually, he didn't know *how* to be sick. He had always been well. The pain subsided, and he took the train back to Chicago. The Party's Political Committee met there on Sunday, February 27—the last meeting that Ruthenberg attended.

Foster was there, and noticed that Ruthenberg's face was pale and strained, though he did not complain of pain.

"You look sick, Charley," Foster said, sympathetically.

"Yes, Bill, I'm kind of under the weather," Ruthenberg answered, smiling wanly. But he was jotting down notes, planning to write a new party statement.

A couple of hours later he collapsed, and was taken directly to the American Hospital for an emergency appendectomy. He died three days afterward, Wednesday, March 2, at 11:00 a.m., of acute peritonitis. The headline of the *Daily Worker* on March 3 was "Ruthenberg Is Dead."

It was impossible and unbelievable, and many who read the news said so, but it was true. Thousands of party members and their families, and hundreds of friends and liberals, mourned his untimely passing. Messages of sympathy and condolence came from the Debs family, American Civil Liberties Union attorney Arthur Garfield Hays, noted churchman Professor Harry F. Ward, Unitarian pastor Rev. David Rhys Williams, Professor Ellen Hayes of Wellesley College, and—in a cable from Moscow—William D. Haywood, and many others. Cablegrams honoring Ruthenberg came from the Communist Parties of the Soviet Union, China, Mexico and other Latin American republics, Germany, England, France, Italy, Canada, Poland, Austria, Czechoslovakia, and other countries.

Ruthenberg's body lay in state at the Ashland Boulevard Auditorium, Chicago, where, on Sunday, March 6, Foster and others spoke. A large crowd took part in the funeral march to the Graceland Cemetery Chapel, where the body was cremated and the ashes placed in a bronze urn.

The urn was taken by train to New York, where a memorial meeting was held Wednesday evening, March 9. So great was the outpouring of New York workers to pay their last respects to a fallen leader that Carnegie Hall, Central Opera House and the New Star Casino—seating in all nearly 10,000—where the memorial meetings were held, were filled to capacity. The long list of speakers, who had to be shunted from hall to hall, included—besides Ruthenberg's co-workers—his old friend, Bishop William Montgomery Brown, who, wearing a black robe and a red cross, gave an eloquent address at each of the meetings.[7]

All over the country, in such Ohio towns as Cleveland, Warren, Toledo, Canton, Youngstown, Columbus, where he was personally known to thousands, and outside of Ohio, in Detroit, Grand Rapids, Milwaukee, Philadelphia, Baltimore, Pittsburgh, San Francisco, Los Angeles, Seattle, St. Paul, Minneapolis, Duluth, Buffalo, Boston, Washington, D. C.—from coast to coast, in city after city, memorial meetings for Ruthenberg were held.

Some three years earlier Ruthenberg had been elected to the Presidium of the Communist International; now the Communist Party of the Soviet Union requested that his ashes be sent there for burial, and this was done. Today his remains rest beside those of other heroes and leaders, including his fellow American, John Reed, who died there in 1920 at the age of thirty-three.

The last recording that Ruthenberg made on the office dictaphone for publication was a statement for the annual International Woman's Day, March 8, which he had prepared in advance and dictated. It was "played back" to a meeting on that day—six days after the speaker's death.

He was a truly great man.[8] He was forty-four at his death, and had devoted the best years of his life to the working class movement: ten years in the Socialist Party, and eight years—the first and stormiest—in the Communist Party.[9] "Whoso fadeth and dieth," wrote William Morris, Ruthenberg's favorite poet, referring to those who fall in the struggle for socialism, "yet his deed shall still prevail." And his deeds *have* prevailed. The Day he looked forward to *is* coming. His life was a victory.

NOTES AND REFERENCES

Chapter 1

1. Records of the Trinity Evangelical Church of Cleveland, Vol. II, p. 425, entry number 1611.
2. Samuel J. Orth, *History of Cleveland,* Vol. I, 1910.
3. Two bookstores, now out of existence, were then located in the Old Arcade, 420 Superior Ave., N. E.—one in Room 48, the other in Room 505.
4. Berkey and Dyke's Business College, E. 9th St. and Prospect Ave., merged later with the Spencerian Business School and is now the Dyke School of Commerce, in Standard Building.
5. An allusion to "A Message to Garcia," by Elbert Hubbard, *The Philistine,* March, 1900. Lieut. Andrew Summers Rowan communicated with General Calixto Garcia in Cuba, April 24, 1898, in the Spanish-American War.

Chapter 2

1. Ben Hanford, *Fight for Your Life,* 1909. Wilshire Publishing Co., New York. The opening story. "The Jimmie Higginses," first appeared in the New York *Call.*
2. Herbert M. Morais and William Cahn, *Gene Debs: The Story of a Fighting American,* New York, 1948, pp. 79-90.
3. The authorities Ruthenberg cited may be identified as follows: Karl Marx (1818-1883), *Capital;* Ernest Belfort Bax (1854-1926), *Socialism, Its Growth and Outcome,* 1894 (written in collaboration with William Morris); William Morris (1834-1896). British socialist poet; Albert E. F. Schaeffle (1831-1903), *The Quintessence of Socialism* (7th edition translated into English by Bernard Bosanquet, London, 1901). The opponents he mentions were William Graham (1839-1911), a Scottish economist and professor, *Socialism New and Old* (2nd edition published in New York, 1891); and Robert Flint (1838-1910), Scottish theologian, *Socialism* (2nd edition published in 1908).
4. Alexander Trachtenberg, *The Heritage of Gene Debs,* New York, 1929; 1947; 1956.
5. Charlotte Todes, *William H. Sylvis and the National Labor Union,* New York, 1942, p. 86.
6. *Ibid.,* p. 73.
7. *Proceedings,* National Convention of the Socialist Party, 1908, pp. 300-306.
8. *The International Socialist Review,* Chicago, 1909-10, carried Lida Parce's "Woman and the Socialist Philosophy," Rose Strunsky's "The Relation of Socialism to the Woman Question," etc.
9. Morris Friedman, *The Pinkerton Labor Spy,* New York, 1907; also William D. Haywood, *Bill Haywood's Book,* New York, 1929, pp. 190-9.

10. A reference to the adverse Supreme Court decision in the AFL Danbury Hatters case in 1908.
11. The N. Y. women's dressmakers' strike (ILGWU), from Nov., 1909, to Feb., 1910. Louis Levine, *The Women's Garment Workers,* New York, 1924, pp. 144 *ff*.
12. The IWW conducted a free speech fight in Spokane in 1909. Paul Frederick Brissenden, *The I. W. W.: A Study of American Syndicalism,* New York, 1920, p. 265.
13. *The Cleveland Citizen,* March 26, 1910.
14. *Encyclopedia Britannica,* 9th edition (available in 1910), Thomas Kirkup. "Socialism" (Vol. XXII): "And it should be said that the ethics of socialism are closely akin to the ethics of Christianity, if not identical with them."
15. *The Cleveland Citizen,* May 21, 1910.

Chapter 3

1. *The Cleveland Citizen,* Oct. 14, 1911, says 100,000 leaflets were to be distributed on Sunday, Oct. 15.
2. *The Cleveland Citizen,* August 26, 1911.
3. *Ohio Socialist Bulletin,* May, 1911.
4. *The Cleveland Citizen,* May 27, June 10, June 17, and Dec. 9, 1911.
5. Nathan Fine, *Labor and Farmer Parties in the United States, 1828-1928.* New York, 1928, pp. 223-5.
6. Government Printing Office, fiftieth number, *Statistical Abstract of the United States,* 1928, pp. 287 and 780; *Ohio Guide,* New York, 1940.
7. Moody's *Industrials,* 1954, p. 1936; Anna Rochester, *Rulers of America,* New York, 1936, p. 51.
8. Selig Perlman and Philip Taft, *History of Labor in the United States, 1896-1932*: Vol. IV, *Labor Movements,* 1935, New York, pp. 138-142; Horace Davis, *Labor and Steel,* New York, 1933, p. 236.
9. Alexander Trachtenberg, editor, *The American Labor Year Book,* published by the Rand School of Social Science, New York, 1916, pp. 51 and 269; Horace Davis, *op. cit.,* p. 239.
10. Selig Perlman and Philip Taft, *op. cit.,* p. 342.
11. *Reports* of Commission on Industrial Relations, Frank P. Walsh, chairman, Washington, D. C., 1914, 1915, 1916, comprising thirteen volumes in all. The Commission was created August 12, 1912, and proceeded to hold public hearings in a dozen cities from New York to San Francisco, at which more than three hundred representatives of labor organizations and employers associations, spokesmen from big corporations as well as the Socialist Party and the Industrial Workers of the World, offered oral and documented testimony. The conclusions of the Commission were given in two *Reports* (1914 and 1915), and the testimony filled eleven volumes (1916). The report was the greatest exposé of labor oppression ever made in the United States. There was "a rapidly growing feeling," the *Report* (1915) noted, "that redress for injustice and oppression cannot be secured through existing governmental institutions."

CHAPTER 4

1. *Proceedings,* Socialist Party Convention, 1912, pp. 82-87; Ira Kipnis, *The American Socialist Movement, 1897-1912,* Columbia University Press, New York, 1952, p. 218.
2. William Z. Foster, *From Bryan to Stalin,* New York, 1937, pp. 71-2; and *American Trade Unionism,* New York, 1947, pp. 15 *ff.*
3. *Proceedings,* Socialist Party Convention, 1912, pp. 79--80.
4. William Z. Foster, *American Trade Unionism,* pp. 16-18; *Misleaders of Labor,* New York, 1927, pp. 31-2; and *History of the Communist Party of the United States,* New York, 1952, pp. 99-103 and 119-126.
5. Alexander Trachtenberg, *The Heritage of Gene Debs,* 1929; 1947; 1956. See Introduction.
6. *Proceedings,* Socialist Party Congress, 1910, pp. 106 *ff.*
7. Art Young, *Art Young, His Life and Times,* New York, 1939. p. 286.
8. *International Socialist Review,* June, 1912.
9. Wm. D. Haywood and Frank Bohn, *Industrial Socialism,* Chas. H. Kerr & Co., Chicago, 1911, p. 57.
10. Wm. English Walling, J. G. Phelps Stokes, Jessie Wallace Hughan, Harry W. Laidler, *The Socialism of Today,* New York, 1916, pp. 383-385.
11. Wm. D. Haywood, *Bill Haywood's Book,* New York, 1929, p. 258.
12. *Proceedings,* Socialist Party Convention, 1912, pp. 86-91.
13. *Ibid,* pp. 144-6.
14. Alexander Trachtenberg, *op. cit.*
15. *Ibid.*
16. Jessie W. Hughan, "The Socialist Movement in the United States," *The American Labor Year Book,* Alexander Trachtenberg, editor, Rand School of Social Science, New York, 1916.

CHAPTER 5

1. *Cleveland Citizen,* Oct. 5, 1912.
2. *World Almanac,* New York, 1914, p. 763.
3. *Cleveland Socialist,* April 6, 1912; reprinted in *Voices of Revolt,* No. X, *Speeches and Writings of Charles E. Ruthenberg,* New York, 1928.
4. *Ohio Socialist Bulletin,* Oct., 1912.
5. Ira Kipnis. *The American Socialist Movement, 1897-1912,* 1952.
6. *The International Socialist Review.* Feb., 1913, p. 623, carried a "resolution of protest" against the recall of Haywood, signed by many prominent persons, including Osmond K. Fraenkel, John Sloan, Bertha W. Howe, Louis B. Boudin, and Walter Lippmann.
7. Allan L. Benson, *The Bomb Shell That Henry Ford Fired,* 1914.
8. The Young People's Socialist League advertised in the *Cleveland Citizen,* Sept. 26, 1914: "Wouldn't you be interested in a cross country hike? . . . Let Comrade Ruthenberg show you the country."
9. *Cleveland Citizen,* May 24, 1913.
10. Ella Reeve Bloor, *We Are Many,* New York, 1940, p. 99.
11. John Reed, "What About Mexico?" *Masses,* New York, June, 1914; John Stuart, *The Education of John Reed,* New York, 1955, pp. 47-73.

CHAPTER 6

1. For the full text of the Basle resolution, see Alexander Trachtenberg, editor, *The American Socialists and the War,* Rand School of Social Science, New York, June, 1917, p. 48. Also V. I. Lenin, *Collected Works,* Vol. 18, *The Imperialist War,* New York, 1930, p. 469.
2. Quoted in *Voices of Revolt,* No. IX, *Speeches of Eugene V. Debs,* edited by Alexander Trachtenberg, 1928, pp. 63-5.
3. Among the books Ruthenberg read and spoke of around this time, old friends say, were Anderson-Nexo's *Pelle the Conqueror,* Eugene Woods' *Back Home,* and H. G. Wells' *The Passionate Friends.*
4. *International Socialist Review,* August, 1914.
5. Andre Tridon's translation, Progress Printing Company, 49 Dudley St., Boston, Mass. No year is given on the title page, but Lenin's preface for the American edition is dated May 9, 1917.
6. Joseph North, *Robert Minor: Artist and Crusader,* New York, 1956.
7. John Reed, *Insurgent Mexico,* New York, 1914. This book appeared two years before the Pershing-Villa episode. It informed the American people, beforehand, of the actual conditions in Mexico.

CHAPTER 7

1. *Cleveland Citizen,* March 31, 1917.
2. Ray Ginger, *The Bending Cross,* New Brunswick, 1949, p. 342.
3. Two years earlier, at conferences in Zimmerwald and Kienthal, Switzerland, Lenin had worked to strengthen a resolution against the war, and added his signature to it along with other internationalist and anti-war Socialists.
4. The Milwaukee *Leader* editorial was quoted in the Socialist Party *Bulletin* (national organ), April, 1919.
5. *The World Almanac,* New York, 1918. The unusually high vote for Hillquit helped to elect ten State Assemblymen, seven city Aldermen, and one municipal judge.
6. *The New Republic,* Dec. 1, 1917, p. 125. Hillquit's letter was a reply to William Hard, who in the previous issue (Nov. 24) had demanded from Hillquit answers to three questions, including, "If there were a referendum on withdrawal from the war, which way would you vote?" Hillquit's answer was "I would vote no."
7. *The Class Struggle,* May-June, 1918.
8. Alexander Trachtenberg, editor, *The American Socialists and the War, op. cit.,* pp. 38 *ff.*
9. From William Morris, "The Voice of Toil." Quoting from memory, Ruthenberg transposed a couple of words.
10. *Guilty? Of What?* published in Cleveland, August, 1917, by the Socialist Party of Ohio, contains the chief speeches made during the trial.
11. Philip S. Foner, *History of the Labor Movement in the United States,* New York, Vol. II, 1955, p. 426.
12. The FBI was then known as the U.S. Secret Service; Max Lowenthal, *The Federal Bureau of Investigation,* New York, 1950.

Chapter 8

1. *Cleveland Citizen,* April 14, 1917.
2. *N. Y. Times,* April 25, 1917.
3. *N. Y. Times,* May 2, 1917.
4. In nearby Toledo, Socialist Councilman Bruce Smith, friend of Ruthenberg, was removed from the office he had been elected to.
5. *Socialist News,* June 15, 1918; *Voices of Revolt,* No. IX, *Speeches of Eugene V. Debs,* pp. 71-3.
6. Quoted by Herbert M. Morais and William Cahn in *Gene Debs: The Story of a Fighting American,* New York, 1948, p. 103.
7. See *Socialist News,* July 27 and October 19, 1918, for reference to A. Phillips Randolph and Chandler Owen. On Aug. 3, 1918, this paper reported that Ross D. Brown, Negro Socialist speaker, was holding daily street meetings in Cleveland. The issues of June 30 and Oct. 19, 1918, scheduled lectures by John Reed.
8. The *Socialist News* erroneously said the series would begin on Dec. 8. It began on Dec. 7, 1918, and ended Feb. 27, 1919.
9. Lenin's *Letter* had reportedly been published earlier in *The Internationalist,* Boston. All such early versions of the *Letter* were inaccurate and incomplete. First correct and complete translation was brought out by International Publishers in 1934.

Chapter 9

1. Bakers Union, Local 56, staged a one-day strike in order to march. Ladies Garment Workers (*Cleveland Plain Dealer,* May 1, 1919) "expressly permitted members to attend and officers said yesterday 3,000 will march."
2. The clubs were supplied, according to the Socialists, by the Peerless Auto Company plant.
3. Cleveland *Citizen,* May 10, 1919; Ohio *Socialist,* June 11, 1919.
4. Ohio *Socialist,* July 2, 1919.
5. New York *Call,* July 20, 1919.
6. Lusk Committee Report, New York State, *Revolutionary Radicalism* (4 vols.), Albany, 1920.
7. *People v. Ferguson et al,* 234 N. Y. 159. Appeal argued June 7, decided July 12, 1922. Conviction reversed and new trial ordered. New York County Lawyers Association: First Dept. 1921, Case 1296, Vol. 209; 1922, Vol. 65.
8. *The Schneiderman Case,* introduction by Carol King, American Committee for Protection of Foreign Born, New York, 1943.
9. New York *World,* March 27, 1922.
10. Judge Bartow S. Weeks died while Ruthenberg was in prison.
11. Ex-Warden Lewis E. Lawes, in a letter on War Production Board stationery, Feb. 8, 1944, refers to Ruthenberg's "splendid personality" and "fine mind."
12. New York *Call.* Aug. 24, 1922.
13. Chicago *Tribune,* Aug. 22 and 24, 1922, on Department of Justice role.
14. At New York Public Library: *American Civil Liberties Cases,* 1922, Vol. I, "Memorandum on the Communist Cases," Sept. 26, 1922.

15. *Workers Defense Union,* New York, Nov., 1920, statements by twelve lawyers, including Felix Frankfurter, Francis Fisher Kane, Frank P. Walsh, Roscoe Pound; Clarissa S Ware, *The American Foreign-Born Workers,* New York, July, 1923; and Louis F. Post, *The Deportation Delirium of 1920,* Chicago, 1923.
16. *The Liberator,* February, 1923.

CHAPTER 10

1. The New York *Call,* first socialist daily in English in the United States, existed from May, 1908, to October, 1923. The daily New York *Leader,* which took its place, became the weekly *New Leader.* The Chicago *Daily Socialist,* founded early in 1912, became the weekly Chicago *Socialist.*
2. *The Liberator,* January, 1923.
3. William Z. Foster, *History of the Communist Party of the United States,* New York, p. 217.
4. *Ibid.,* pp. 221-223; 269-275.
5. *Daily Worker,* November 27, 1926.
6. *Daily Worker,* February 5, 1927; *Stalin's Speeches on the American Question;* New York, 1928.
7. Bishop William Montgomery Brown, of the Protestant Episcopal Church in the United States, author of *My Heresy,* Galion, Ohio, 1925; *Communism and Christianism,* 1928; *Science and History for Boys and Girls, 1932;* and other writings.
8. Alex Bittelman, *Milestones in the History of the Communist Party,* August, 1937.
9. Elisabeth Gurley Flynn, *Debs, Haywood, Ruthenberg,* a biographical essay, New York, September, 1939.

LIST OF SELECTED WRITINGS
BY CHARLES E. RUTHENBERG

A. Pamphlets

Are We Growing Toward Socialism? Spring, 1917.

Guilty? Of What? (Speeches in court, Ohio: C. E. Ruthenberg and Alfred Wagenknecht), Fall, 1917.

After the War—What? December, 1918. (Entire edition lost, but recovered in extant copies of *Socialist News.*)

A Communist Trial (Speeches in court, New York: Ruthenberg and Ferguson), Fall, 1920.

The Second Convention (Report of the Central Executive Committee, Workers Party of America), 1922.

The Bridgman Trial (Speeches in court, Michigan: Ruthenberg and Foster), Fall, 1923, or Winter, 1924.

Why Every Worker Should Be a Communist and Join the Workers Party, 1923.

The Party Constitution (Introduction by Ruthenberg), various editions in 1923, 1924.

The Farmer-Labor United Front, May, 1924.

The Fourth National Convention (Report of the Central Executive Committee, Workers Party of America), August 21-30, 1925.

From the Third Through the Fourth Convention of the Workers (Communist) Party of America, Fall, 1925.

The Paris Commune (in historical pictures, Introduction by Ruthenberg), Spring, 1926.

The Workers (Communist) Party: What It Stands For; Why Workers Should Join, 1926. (This was a revision of the 1923 pamphlet listed above).

B. Magazine and Newspaper Articles and Leaflets

"You Will Pay in Blood and Suffering," anti-war leaflet, April 1, 1917.

"This Is Not a War for Freedom," anti-war speech, May 27, 1917.

"Greeting to the October Revolution," leaflet, Nov., 1917.

"On the Threshold of the New World," *Socialist News,* April 27, 1918 (May Day message from Canton Workhouse).

"Forward, March!" leaflet, January, 1919 (Written immediately after release from Canton Workhouse).

"The Bankruptcy of Democracy," *Socialist News,* Feb. 1, 1919.

"Who Are the Murderers?" leaflet, early May, 1919 (Reply to the assault on the May Day parade, and to the frame-up murder charge against him).

"The Communist Party and Its Tasks," *The Communist,* July, 1921.

"The Need for Open Work," *The Communist,* Aug., 1921.

"Communism in the Open Again," *The Liberator,* Feb., 1923.

"An Open Challenge," *The Liberator,* March, 1923.

"Role of the Workers Party," *The Liberator,* July, 1923.

"The Revolutionary Party," *The Liberator,* Jan. 1924.

"Seven Years of the Communist Party," *The Workers Monthly,* Sept., 1926.

"Two Supreme Court Decisions," *Daily Worker,* Nov. 9, 1926.

"First Signs of a Downward Trend in Industry," *Daily Worker,* Feb. 5, 1927.

INDEX